Politics in Public Service Advertising on Television

David L. Paletz
Roberta E. Pearson
Donald L. Willis

The Praeger Special Studies program—utilizing the most modern and efficient book production techniques and a selective worldwide distribution network—makes available to the academic, government, and business communities significant, timely research in U.S. and international economic, social, and political development.

Politics in Public Service Advertising on Television

PRAEGER SPECIAL STUDIES IN U.S. ECONOMIC, SOCIAL, AND POLITICAL ISSUES

Praeger Publishers New York London

Library of Congress Cataloging in Publication Data

Paletz, David L 1934-
Politics in public service advertising on television.

(Praeger special studies in U.S. economic, social, and political issues)
Includes bibliographical references and index.
1. Advertising, Public service—United States.
2. Television advertising—United States. I. Pearson, Roberta E., joint author. II. Willis, Donald L., joint author. III. Title.
HF6146.T42P34 659.13 76-24363
ISBN 0-275-23880-6

PRAEGER PUBLISHERS
200 Park Avenue, New York, N.Y. 10017, U.S.A.

Published in the United States of America in 1977
by Praeger Publishers, Inc.

Printed in the United States of America

For my mother and the
memory of my father
(D.L.P.)

To the memory
of my mother
(R.E.P.)

To my parents and
my Durham family
(D.L.W.)

ACKNOWLEDGMENTS

Our debts are many. We acknowledge first our numerous respondents in government, private nonprofit organizations, advertising agencies, public interest groups, and the networks who discussed their work with us. Without their time and candor this book could not have been written.

Our colleagues in Political Science at Duke University, abetted by enlightened administrators, sustain a serene environment which encourages intellectual passions no matter how untoward. The staff of Duke's Media Center (disbanded) and Computer Center performed their technical tasks with facility and dispatch.

At the American University in Washington, D.C., Dean of the School of Government and Public Affairs A. Lee Fritschler enthusiastically ensured that we received the necessary technical and financial support. Professor Coralie Bryant gave sustenance and friendship. Jane Takeuchi, Terry Shaeffer, and the staff of the Media Center helped immeasurably with the logistics of tracing and recording fugitive public service advertisements.

When our assumption that a significant research project could be undertaken and completed without any external funding proved too optimistic, we applied to the National Endowment for the Humanities for a Youthgrant. The Endowment bestowed a modest sum enabling us to complete our research. It should be noted that we actually returned unspent funds to NEH, an action possibly unique in the history of grantsmanship. Of course, our findings and conclusions do not necessarily represent the view of the Endowment.

David Eisenberg worked with us in the research until his political and social concerns led him abroad. Meri-Li Douglas and Janet A. Colm labored mightily typing versions of the manuscript. Anita Schoomaker did the index. We give thanks to and for you all.

Our special gratitude goes to Professor W. Phillips Davison of Columbia University. As editor of the *Public Opinion Quarterly,* he encouraged the senior author's forays into the relationships of politics and the media. We first presented our public service advertising findings at his panel at the annual meeting of the American Association for Public Opinion Research. Professor Davison also recommended our publisher.

The insistence of our publisher on a sedate title probably saved us from ourselves. It also leaves us with "Another Opiate for the People," "Packaging the People," and "See Spots Run" to conjure with for future manuscripts.

Having acknowledged this legion of contributors, we feel it only just to blame its members for whatever errors of fact the book contains. Errors of interpretation are the fault of our friends and colleagues who should have saved us from them. Scintillating insights and felicitous phrases are our responsibility.

Finally, with admiration and love, we embrace our families, while noting that if Darcy Paletz were less liberated and Gabriel Michael Paletz and Susannah Batyah Felicity Paletz did not insist on playing the "Magic Flute" continuously, this book would have been completed much sooner.

CONTENTS

Politics in Public Service Advertising on Television

CHAPTER

1

INTRODUCTION

"Ladies and gentlemen, I am suggesting nothing less than an effective campaign to improve public understanding of our American economic system,"[1] said then Commerce Secretary Frederick B. Dent in a speech to the board of directors of the Advertising Council. Shortly thereafter, the Commerce Department provided the Council with $239,000 allocated from the Office of Minority Business Enterprise and the Economic Development Administration; and the Advertising Council started raising from the private sector some of the remaining $1.25 million it was estimated the campaign would cost.

In politics, rhetoric often succeeds decisions; it did so here. Secretary Dent's challenge culminated discussions between Commerce and the Council. Initiated by the Council, they also involved Compton Advertising, the agency that would receive the contract from the Council to handle the campaign.[2]

The campaign is scheduled to last from three to five years. It consists of two parts: first, a now completed survey of the attitudes of Americans towards their economic system; second, the preparation of a 25-page booklet purportedly explaining the system. To bring this publication to the attention of the American people and ensure its distribution, the Advertising Council and Compton are using the panoply of available media—most prominently, television and radio. For television, color film spots of assorted lengths have been produced and distributed to the three networks and hundreds of stations throughout the United States. The stations are urged to show them without charge as public service announcements.

The ostensible purpose of the booklet is to educate the adult high-school graduate who is supposedly baffled by the complexity of economics. But witness how the booklet begins:

> The United States in its 200 years of existence has grown to be the economic wonder of the world, bringing forth a richness from its

> farms and factories unprecedented in all history. During this period, we have also enjoyed a unique form of democratic government that has been an inspiration to freedom-seeking peoples throughout the world. As we now celebrate the Bicentennial Anniversary of our independence, we should be aware of the very important connection between our economic progress and the vitality of our democratic form of government.
>
> This booklet presents some of the economic principles upon which America's prosperity has been built, and upon which we can continue to progress during the years ahead.[3]

This is advocacy disguised as description: an attempt, at least in part, to persuade us to appreciate the benefits and accomplishments of corporate capitalism and to oppose changing the economic system that assertedly brings them.

Here is a private organization, joining with a government agency, spending vast sums of money, some of it from the taxpayers, using all the media, especially television, for purposes akin to propaganda. A strange business. What is the Advertising Council? How has it achieved such intimate connections with government and the media? Why do advertising agencies volunteer their services to undertake campaigns through the Council? Above all, what exactly are public service announcements? how do they affect us? and why should we care?

Public service advertisements (PSAs) are spots of 10, 20, 30, or 60 seconds, sponsored by nonprofit agencies, and aired free of charge by broadcasters.* An official definition can be found in the Federal Communications Commission license renewal form:

> A public service announcement (PSA) is any announcement (including network) for which no charge is made and which promotes programs, activities, or services of federal, state or local governments (e.g., recruiting, sales of bonds, etc.) or the programs, activities or services of non-profit organizations (e.g., UGF, Red Cross blood donations, etc.), and other announcements regarded as serving community interests, excluding time signals, routine weather announcements and promotional announcements.[4]

No one in the academic community has conducted an extensive study of public service announcements, which remain ubiquitous but unexamined.†

---

*Although PSAs appear on the radio and in print media, this book is solely concerned with television. A complete study of public service advertising in all three media would require far more time and resources. Although the limitation is mainly methodological, there is also theoretical justification: television is the medium that reached the largest audience and on which most people rely for information concerning the outside world.

†The spots are referred to interchangeably as public service announcements or public service advertisements. Although the FCC officially defines the spots as announcements, we call them public service advertisements. "Announcements" is a neutral term implying that PSAs are in the public interest. As will be shown later, many PSAs are directed more toward furthering the interests of those producing them than toward aiding the public. Thus, "advertisements" is more descriptive.

Given the amount of television watched by the average person in the United States, it is reasonable to assume that most viewers have been exposed to a great many PSAs, yet very little is known about the process by which the spots are produced and eventually aired or what they communicate to the American public. Scattered articles, both scholarly and nonscholarly, have discussed various aspects of the subject, but this book is the first comprehensive study of PSAs.

Television public service advertising will be approached on two levels: the operations of production, distribution, and airing; and a more speculative discussion of the values espoused in the spots and their political relevance. On the first level, a framework is needed to provide a method of examining the operations of the public service advertising business. This framework is predicated on two basic facts: first, public service air time is a relatively scarce commodity—there are only so many spaces available for PSAs; second, America contains far more institutions, organizations, agencies, and groups than there is time for the PSAs they might produce. Obviously there must be a winnowing process whereby relatively few groups request air time, and of these still fewer receive it. We call this process "funneling."

Many national, state, and local nonprofit organizations and national, state, and local government agencies seek PSA access to the media. A group that hopes to use PSAs to further its organizational goals must persuade those controlling the public service advertising process to assist its efforts and to provide air time for its messages. Those entities which either aid or impede a group's progress through the funneling process are advertising agencies, the Advertising Council, the networks, and the local stations. Each of these bases its decision as to whether to accord access upon its perceptions of a group's finances, reputation, credibility, goals, and other organizational attributes.

This book describes the operation of each stage of the funneling process, the role that each of the four controlling entities plays, and the activities of other organizations on the periphery of the process.

Merely being familiar with the nature of the funneling process is of little value unless this methodological framework provides a way to deal with important questions concerning the nature and organization of public service advertising. One basic question is, "Which groups receive air time?" A corollary is, of course, "Which groups do not receive air time?" Answering these questions requires an analysis of each stage of the funneling process. We therefore look at the decision makers in the process, hoping to discover the values they hold, the goals toward which they are striving, and their general feelings about the nature of their jobs and the industry or profession of which they are a part. The decision makers are involved in the institutional and bureaucratic structures. What are the norms of the structures, and what pressures do they exert on the individual participants? What are the other variables that impinge upon the decision makers' activities? The next four chapters present data concerning the operation of the funneling process and how it acts to include some groups and exclude others.

A group that has been aided by those controlling the public service advertising process must face a final obstacle. It may fail when its PSAs are actually aired and received by an audience. Will the audience perceive, accept, and respond to the message of the PSA? Will it act in accord with the hopes of the producers? Will members of the audience change their attitudes or behavior, donate money, volunteer their services, or do whatever else they are urged to do? Chapter 6 discusses the immediate, short-range impact and effectiveness of PSAs.

The seventh chapter examines the overt results of the funneling process through a content analysis of a sample of PSAs broadcast in two cities. We try to determine which groups actually produce PSAs appearing on the air, the subjects the PSAs cover, the audience the messages appeal to, and the techniques used to increase PSA efficacy.

Chapter 8 begins the speculative heart of the book. We dissect the explicit and implicit messages contained in PSAs and connect them to the American political system. Do PSAs promote consensus or cleavage? Do they encourage affective or instrumental orientations to governmental and nongovernmental institutions? What sort of political participation if any, do they stimulate? What are the implications of our analysis for democracy in the United States?

Chapter 12 discusses the prospects for change and the possibilities of including some of the excluded individuals and groups. The last chapter contains our conclusions.

Four methodological tools have been used in this study. To compile data concerning the operations of the funneling process, interviews were conducted with numerous people in government, nonprofit organizations, advertising agencies, networks, stations, and the Advertising Council. Because we often promised anonymity to induce candor, many of our respondents and informants are not individually identified.[5] A questionnaire was sent to 177 television stations, of which 106—approximately 15 percent of the country's 700 television stations—responded. To gain some measure of the impact of PSAs, a telephone poll was conducted in Washington, D.C., and Durham, North Carolina, with 100 responses obtained from each city. To examine the end result of the funneling process, a content analysis of 94 PSAs aired during a one-week period on a station in Washington, D.C., and a station in Durham, North Carolina, was conducted.

Through these diverse methods, plus industry, persistence, and luck, we have managed to penetrate the nether world of public service advertising. We emerge with an appreciation of the complexity of the process and the ingenuity of the participants, and with a realization of the existence of what could be called propaganda in America.

NOTES

1. The speech is reprinted in U.S., Congress, House Committee on Government Operations, Subcommittee on Commerce, Consumer, and Monetary Affairs, *Oversight*

Hearing on Commerce Department Payment to the National Advertising Council for Promotion of the Free Enterprise System, 94th Cong., 1st sess., July 30, 1975, p. 43.

2. Letter from the Deputy Comptroller General of the United States to Congressman Benjamin S. Rosenthal, December 3, 1975, pp. 2-4. Congressman Rosenthal (D., N.Y.) and other members of the subcommittee tried to establish a more conspiratorial explanation during the hearings on the campaign and the federal government's involvement. They contended that the original idea was enunciated by Howard J. Morgens, then chairman of Procter and Gamble, at an Advertising Council dinner in 1973, in which he gave a speech entitled "The Profit Motive and the Public Interest." Procter and Gamble is America's largest national advertiser. Its executives gave amply to the successful 1972 presidential reelection campaign of Richard M. Nixon. In arranging for the Commerce Department to help fund the campaign, the congressmen contended, Secretary Dent was responding to Morgens' initiative. They pointed out that Compton Advertising is employed by Procter and Gamble. The connections were admitted but collusion steadfastly denied by representatives of the Commerce Department and the Advertising Council who testified at the hearings. See *Oversight Hearing,* pp. 10, 15. Congressman Rosenthal has been a persistent critic and antagonist of the Advertising Council; we discuss his activities in more detail in Chapter 12.

3. *The American Economic System and Your Part in It,* The Advertising Council, Inc., and the Department of Commerce, n.d., p. 1.

4. U.S., Federal Communications Commission, *Broadcast Application,* November 1974, Sec. IV-A, p. 8.

5. Depending upon the sensitivity of the subject under discussion, some interviews were tape-recorded, at others notes were taken, and at still others we made notes when the interview was over. Consequently, the quotations may not always contain the exact words used by our respondents.

CHAPTER

2

THE ADVERTISING COUNCIL AND ITS FRIENDS

It is widely believed among those involved in public service advertising that Advertising Council sanction of a campaign is "golden, absolutely golden." This is so for two reasons: First, if a group is lucky enough to become one of the approximately 25 major campaigns the Council undertakes each year (there were 27 in 1975), it will have a complete public service effort developed for it by one of the country's leading advertising agencies and be responsible only for expenses incurred in the production of the advertising material. Second, the Advertising Council will distribute all the materials (formats for magazine and newspaper advertisements, car cards for transit advertising, taped radio spots), including sending the television spots to every station in the country. These stations are likely to air the spots bearing the Council imprimatur because, according to a prominent advertising executive, they "know it has been checked out, it's not objectionable to too many people, and they know it's good, creative material." The Council also provides assistance to some groups which do not obtain major campaign status by listing them in the *Public Service Advertising Bulletin*. This is published bimonthly by the Council and reaches roughly 13,000 media outlets. A listing in this bulletin implies that the Council approves of the organization and is in agreement with its goals. Station personnel are often more receptive to groups so listed. In 1975, according to the Council, 49 groups (51 campaigns) were included in the bulletin.

The Council claims to originate roughly 40 percent of all the public service advertising shown in the country,[1] including television and radio, magazines, newspapers, billboards, and transit signs. In 1975, the time and space contributed by the various media would have cost $591,808,211 if purchased by commercial advertisers.[2] Since the Council's inception in 1942, approximately

$8 billion worth of time and space have been donated to its campaign materials.[3] Furthermore, according to the Council, in 1975 its television spots were shown 5,510 times by the networks and over 1 million times by the individual local stations.[4]

It is clear that a great deal of the public service advertising reaching the American people originates with the Advertising Council. A group that obtains Council support is virtually assured of wide public exposure, so this support is a much valued and highly contested commodity. The Council received numerous requests for support, of which only a select few became major campaigns—that is, were given the services of an advertising agency and have had their material distributed by the Council. Why are these groups chosen? The answer lies in the structure and operation of the Council: its personnel, sources of funds, organizational apparatus; and in its relationship with the networks, advertising agencies, and governments.

THE COUNCIL'S HISTORY AND STRUCTURE

The Council, then known as the War Advertising Council, was established in March 1942 to marshal the resources of the advertising industry in support of the government's home-front propaganda effort.[5] During the war, the Council handled only government campaigns, working closely with the office of War Information. At the end of World War II, the Council reorganized, cut its ties with the Office of War Information, dropped the word "war" from its name, and undertook nongovernment campaigns.[6] Although the Council maintains close connections with both the executive office of the president and with the Congress, it is formally independent.

The Council describes itself as "a private non-profit corporation supported entirely by American business and the advertising and communications industries."[7] Its sole source of contributed income is from the donations of "business firms and constituent organizations."[8] For the 1972-73 fiscal year, these "business firms and constituent organizations" contributed to an operations budget of $710,281.[9]

The Council consists of a full-time staff of 18; a 79-member board of directors consisting "mainly of advertising agency executives, corporate advertising and public relations directors, and executives from broadcasting, magazines, the business press, newspapers, and transportation and outdoor advertising firms";[10] an industries advisory committee composed "of thirty-eight distinguished business leaders,"[11] and a public policy committee "composed of twenty-two distinguished men and women representing many areas of our society: management, labor, agriculture, medicine, religion, social work, journalism, education and foreign affairs."[12] These bodies decide which groups will become major campaigns of the Council, which will receive bulletin support, and which will be rejected entirely.

All applicants are first screened by the executive staff to ascertain whether the organization and its proposed campaign meet the following criteria of the Council:

(1) That, if the organization requesting Council support is a fund-raising one, the Advertising Council will take into consideration whether or not it currently meets the standards of the National Information Bureau.[13]
(2) That the project be non-commercial, non-partisan politically, and not designed to influence legislation.
(3) That the project be national in scope, or sufficiently national so that the great bulk of the national media audience has an actual or potential interest in it.
(4) That the appeal for support shall be one properly made to Americans generally. The project will not be rejected because it is in the interest of one group if it has wide appeal and national significance.
(5) That the project be of sufficient seriousness and public importance to justify treatment before the national media audience.
(6) That the purpose of the project be such that the advertising methodology can help achieve its objectives.[14]

An organization established by congressional legislation is automatically considered to conform to these standards.[15] Others must meet each of the six criteria before being passed by the executive staff.

The proposed campaign is then scrutinized by the campaigns review committee of the board of directors and then by the entire board of directors, the body that "really runs the Council."[16]

While the proposed campaign is under consideration by the campaigns review committee of the board of directors, it is also being reviewed by the public policy committee, which the president of the Council has referred to as "the Council's chastity belt."[17] This committee is supposed to insure that "Council campaigns are truly in the public interest, and are not commercial or political."[18] Recently the committee has begun making recommendations to the board of directors concerning subjects with which it believes the Council should deal. It is also supposed to "set goals and to establish priorities among these issues."[19] The membership of this committee is not restricted to the communications, advertising, and business worlds, as is that of the board of directors. Among the committee members are an American University law student, the former president of Dartmouth College, the executive director of the National Urban League, and the president of the Rockefeller Foundation. Our impression is that the public policy committee serves mainly in an advisory capacity, while the board of directors has the final say as to which groups are accepted and which are not.

THE DECISION-MAKING PROCESS

We have described the Council's formal decision-making apparatus. As with any organization, however, one cannot assume that, by being familiar with the formal apparatus, one understands the nature of decision making. Other factors enter into Council selection of campaigns, including the application of the criteria, the affiliations and responsibilities of the decision makers, and political input from the current administration in Washington, D.C.

The decision-making bodies use the six criteria as guidelines. However, the criteria can become highly flexible. The United Negro College Fund does not clearly meet either the third or fourth requirement yet the Council felt that it was of sufficient importance to merit full support. The National Alliance of Businessmen's JOBS program is another case in point. In 1968, a member of the Johnson administration reportedly approached the Council prior to passage of the congressional legislation which established the program, asking the Council to develop a campaign for the National Alliance of Businessmen. The Council agreed, in spite of its provision that the program must "not be designed to influence legislation."[20] Moreover, some of the campaigns the Council endorses cannot properly be called nonpartisan, unless one takes a peculiarly narrow view of the term. A "Write Hanoi" campaign reflected the Nixon administration position that U.S. troops would not be withdrawn until all the prisoners were freed.[21]

The Council bears sole responsibility for interpreting and defining the criteria and appears occasionally to use different standards for its decisions; the criteria can become a convenient excuse for excluding a group that is being rejected on other grounds. Furthermore, although the Council claims to make its selections solely on the basis of the written criteria, it is reasonable to assume that other considerations also enter the minds of its decision makers. Not being privy to the deliberations of the decision-making bodies, it is impossible for us to determine exactly what these other considerations might be. However, some insights may be gleaned by examining the positions and responsibilities of decision makers on the various committees of the Council.

The board is composed of chairmen, presidents, and vice-presidents of various businesses, the networks, publishing houses, newspapers, and advertising agencies. Among the business firm members are the senior vice-president of

Sears, Roebuck, a vice-president of IBM, a vice-president of General Mills, a vice-president of Pacific Gas and Electric, a vice-president of the Goodyear Tire and Rubber Company, and a vice-president of Coca Cola. Representing the broadcasters are the chairman of Metromedia, Inc., the president of the Mutual Broadcasting System, and the president of the CBS television stations, among others. Many of the major advertising agencies have representatives on the board, including the president of J. Walter Thompson (the largest advertising agency in the world) and the chairman of Doyle Dane Bernbach Inc.[22] Obviously, many of the members of the board of directors are in positions that would incline them to be receptive to one kind of campaign and, conversely, unreceptive to groups whose goals might run counter to their values and interests. An analysis of the Council's campaigns later in this book tends to confirm this hypothesis.

There is supposedly public input into the process through the much touted public policy committee, but the members of this committee come, in the main, from well-established organizations in the mainstream of American society. Their interests and values most probably are not greatly at variance with those of the Council.

The third factor that impinges on the formal decision-making apparatus is the influence of the current administration on the selection of campaigns. An agency or department of the federal government seeking Council support has an additional hurdle to overcome: it must receive clearance from the White House before approaching the Council. One of the president's assistants coordinates government public service efforts and is also the White House liaison with the Advertising Council. He is charged with deciding which agencies merit Council support and which might be left to try to conduct their own campaigns. President Nixon's first appointee was former football coach Bud Wilkinson. He was succeeded by William F. Rhatican. Rhatican apparently felt that a public service campaign could be more effective if aimed at a target audience. Since one of the Council's criteria is that campaigns be national in scope, Rhatican tended to discourage agencies from requesting Council support.[23] Thus, many potential government requests for Council support were eliminated at this stage, rather than by the Council itself.

White House clearance is the sine qua non for a governmental agency hopeful of becoming one of the major campaigns of the Council. As an executive of the Council put it, "If they [the White House] don't recommend it, we don't touch it." This was attested to by a respondent at the Justice Department connected with the drug abuse campaign, who made a special point of the fact that the Advertising Council agreed to cooperate with his efforts only after the White House became concerned. The indications are that once the White House does approve an agency's proposal, the Council has very few reservations about accepting the campaign for major support. Obviously the Council is responsive to political influence; as Council President Keim stated, "A political atmosphere can color what you do."[24] Thus, one might expect some Council campaigns to reflect social or cultural interests and perhaps even aspects of the political stance of the current occupant of the White House.

Indeed, the Advertising Council has historically maintained a friendly relationship with the White House. In 1945, President Franklin D. Roosevelt indicated his approval of the Council's wartime activities, stating, "It is vitally important that the partnership between business and government, which has so successfully brought information to the people in wartime, continue into the postwar period."[25] Under President Harry S Truman, a government coordinating unit was created to work with the Council. Entitled the Advertising Liaison Division, it was located in the Office of Government Reports.[26]

In 1962, President John F. Kennedy turned to the Council for help in publicizing the then little-known Peace Corps. As has been mentioned, the Johnson administration sought the Council's aid to develop the National Alliance of Businessmen's JOBS program. Working with the Nixon administration, the Council developed such campaigns as "Lock Your Car, Take Your Key," voluntarism, and drug abuse.[27] President Nixon was especially interested in the last, and it was cleared by the White House before being distributed. We may conclude that, with varying degrees of sophistication, each American president since the inception of the Council has recognized its value as a publicity resource for his administration and some of its programs.

A striking example of presidential involvement was the energy conservation campaign, with its slogan "Don't Be Fuelish," which urged Americans to turn off their lights, drive at no more than 55 miles per hour, and keep thermostats no higher than 68 degrees. According to one informant, before the campaign was implemented it had to receive President Nixon's approval. This was granted at a full-scale cabinet meeting where the PSAs were screened to ensure that the administration was depicted favorably in advertising on this issue. The influence of such an administration-Advertising Council combination to achieve speedy access is suggested by the January 1973 announcement that 100 radio and 25 television stations in New York State would be broadcasting such PSAs hourly.[28] That the administration-Advertising Council relationship continued unabated and unabashed with the advent of President Ford is suggested by the appearance of an energy PSA during the 1975 Super Bowl—brought to the vast audience as a public service by the National Football League (commercial time for the event cost over $200,000 per minute). It is confirmed by the dubious WIN campaign.

Sometimes an administration may bypass the Advertising Council entirely and engage in its own PSA campaign. Under the direction of Jeb Magruder, the committee in charge of President Nixon's 1973 inauguration "sent tapes and films to hundreds of radio and television stations, requesting free 10-, 30-, and 60-second spots as public service announcements."[29] The advertisements promoted "inaugural parade tickets and such mementos as the commemorative license plates and the $6 and $45 bronze and silver medals being sold under a sales contract with the Franklin Mint, a private concern."[30] Although the sale of souvenirs appears to be a suspicious use of public service time, the committee said the Federal Communications Commissions had authorized the spots as acceptable public service advertisements. According to Magruder, the committee's marketing campaign was to defray the cost of the four-day ceremony, estimated at up to $4 million. Any surplus would go to charity or future inaugurals.

Aside from presidential sponsorship, there seem to be three ways in which a proposed campaign elicits major support from the Council. Government organizations created through congressional legislation apparently meet Council standards automatically and probably just as automatically receive major support when they want to undertake a campaign. Government agencies with White House clearance seem almost automatically to receive major support. A nongovernmental organization must be approved by the executive staff, the board of directors, and the public policy committee.

CAMPAIGN DEVELOPMENT AND DISTRIBUTION

In order to elucidate the relationships between the Council and advertising and communications elites, we shall now trace the process by which campaigns are conceived, developed, and eventually distributed.

Once the Council has selected a campaign to be one of its major efforts, it asks the American Association of Advertising Agencies, one of its constituent organizations, to choose a volunteer advertising agency. Most of the larger agencies in the country are on the association's waiting list and are eager to obtain a public service account; and many have undertaken several simultaneously.[31] While altruism often motivates such eagerness, there are three ways in which a public service account can be beneficial to an agency.

First, a skillfully handled public service account enhances the agency's reputation and is thus likely to attract commercial accounts. Each campaign conducted by the council requires the services not only of an agency, but of a "volunteer coordinator," chosen by the Association of National Advertisers (another of the Council's constituent organizations) from the communications and advertising divisions of the business corporations that fund the Council. As one advertising agency executive told us, "If you can pitch these companies by your creativity, then you've opened the door for future business." Some agencies also manage to display their names with the advertisement on the screen.

Second, a public service account can salve the consciences of creative people in an agency. As one of their publicity pamphlets states, Young and Rubicam "is well aware of a significant benefit to the agency—giving creative men and women the opportunity to demonstrate their social consciences. 'Without the opportunity for such involvement . . . we could lose our most valued people to the non-business world.' "[32] There is also agreement among people in advertising agencies that a public service account allows more creative freedom than does a commercial account. The public service client is less convinced of its advertising expertise and more willing to allow the writers, artists, and others in the agency to develop a campaign without undue interference. As one executive put it: "The level of acceptance [by the client of agency ideas] is excellent. Things are created with less emasculation." There is stiff competition among agency employees for assignment to public service accounts for the reasons stated above, and one other: PSAs can become very well known. According to a respondent at one agency, "People have made careers, made big names for themselves, in public service advertising."

Third, the agency can calculate what the cost of its services would have been to a commercial client and take the difference between this figure and actual reimbursement as a tax deduction.

Once an agency has been chosen, it works with the volunteer coordinator, the client, and the Council as a task force to develop a campaign. The agency usually assigns only a "skeleton crew," or fewer people than would handle a commercial account. For instance, J. Walter Thompson, which handles the Red Cross account, has only two people from account management, a writer who is a vice-president, a senior art director, one producer, and one traffic man. The agency works up "story boards," or verbal and pictorial descriptions, of the proposed television spots. These are shown to the client, the Council, and the volunteer coordinator, all of whom have to approve them before the spots are produced. Following final approval, the agency contracts with a production house to make the spots. The production house does not usually contribute its services, but charges the client only for the actual production costs. The production house can also take a tax write-off.

Even though the group has obtained the full support of the Council, there is no guarantee that its original concept of the campaign will reach the public. The Council advises the agency concerning what is acceptable to the media. A PSA not only has to appeal to an audience once it is aired, but first has to appeal to broadcasters to ensure that it does get aired. As an advertising agency vice-president stated, "The compromise occurs in someone's mind before they write anything down." In addition, the large number of people involved in campaign development tends to weaken the group's original concept.

Once the spots are produced, they must be distributed and broadcast. A media kit for each of the Council's campaigns is sent to each television station in the country. In addition, the Council attempts to persuade the networks to accept and air its spots. The indications are that while the Council is influential with the networks, the relationship is reciprocal. The Council usually shows the story boards for proposed spots to the networks before actually making the spots. The networks accept the story boards as they are, suggest changes, or indicate that they would not be inclined to air such a PSA. By previewing the spots for the networks, the Council increases the likelihood that the networks will play them. In return, the networks appear often to accept the judgment of the Council as to whether a PSA, once produced, is acceptable for network broadcast. The head of broadcast standards at one network views the Council as a screening organization,"a very helpful instrument in isolating and separating organizations for us." At another network, an executive vice-president said that his company relies heavily on the advice of the Council and accepts it "much of the time," although he went to great lengths to point out that it is not a tool of the Council. Instead, he said, a mutually satisfactory relationship exists because the Council knows the network's standards and conforms to them in order to receive air time.

There would seem to be more involved than just simple conformance to network standards, however. The impression gained from talking to people in the public service advertising business is that they form a close-knit community and that there is much interaction among them. They frequent the same restaurants, belong to the same organizations, and share essentially similar outlooks. There is also some job shuffling. People in advertising agencies may go to work for the Council or for the communications divisions of a nonprofit or government agency, and people in these positions often go to work for advertising agencies or other business firms. They thus develop a web of interconnections upon which the distributors of PSAs can depend to get their material aired. A prominent executive of a PSA sponsor stressed the importance of having professionals handle a campaign for a nonprofit or government agency. "Advertising professionals can be very helpful, with their connections, in getting the media to air the stuff." He explained that "the advertising business is an old-friends business. If you can call up your old friend who is vice-president of CBS and say, 'I'd sure like to have that on the Cronkite program,' then maybe you'll get it."

There are no Federal Communications Commission regulations concerning the number of PSAs to be scheduled, and the networks themselves have no weekly quota. Instead, PSAs generally are aired on a time-available basis, that is,when no commercial advertiser has purchased the space. Promotional spots are usually awarded priority over PSAs for the available space. The number of PSAs thus decreases when the network is doing well with paid advertising or when it is engaged in heavy promotion of its own shows, as at the start of a new season. Since access to network logs is difficult to obtain, there is not much information available about the exact percentage, number, frequency, and time-slotting of Council spots. An executive at one network estimated that of the 50 or more PSAs shown weekly, at least 50 percent have the Advertising Council imprimatur. Our own analysis of the composite week log submitted to the FCC by a CBS affiliate in Washington, D.C. (a location conducive to the abundant airing of PSAs) for 1970 revealed that of 374 PSA spots (some PSAs were shown more than once), 130 were network. Of the 130, at least 80 percent were from the Advertising Council. The evidence suggests, then, that a great many of the PSAs broadcast by the networks are of Advertising Council origin and that a group fortunate enough to become one of the Council's major campaigns is assured of national exposure on all three networks. A PSA aired by a network is also usually carried by all affiliate stations. Since each network has approximately 200 affiliates, a PSA broadcast by a network reaches a massive audience.

Why do the networks show so many Advertising Council PSAs? Our interviews with network personnel revealed that the Advertising Council's bulletins often guide the choice of PSAs to be shown. Indeed, the Council sometimes organizes luncheons with key network decision makers before starting its campaigns. It did so, for example, with its "Don't Be Fuelish" effort.

If a group lacks the Council's official endorsement, its chances of having a PSA shown on a network are helped if it undertakes discussions with network personnel before producing a commercial, uses an influential advertising agency, is a well-known national organization with chapters throughout the United States, and if its message is humanitarian and innocuous. So wary are the networks of controversial PSAs that NBC reportedly will not show any that are religiously oriented. ABC accepts "religious" PSAs, but only if they do not appeal for funds, contain no address to contact, are devoid of ecclesiastical content, and in no way proselytize; advocating brotherhood is acceptable. The networks fear that even the Council's Free Enterprise campaign may cause them problems by opening them up to fairness doctrine complaints.

RESULTS OF COUNCIL PROCEDURES

We have now outlined the process by which campaigns are selected and developed. Inferences concerning the likely results of the Council's structure, method of operations, and relationships with advertising agencies and the networks can be drawn from these data, and illustrative case studies provide support for these inferences. What is the nature of the campaigns the Council sponsors?

The Council says that its campaigns fall under one or more of the following categories: developing human resources, promoting citizen awareness, preserving natural resources, and strengthening the economy.[33]

In 1972-73, the Council conducted 25 major campaigns. Of these, 10 were developed in conjunction with a department or agency of the federal government, and the other 15 were for nonprofit organizations. The ten federal campaigns were: Forest Fire Prevention (Department of Agriculture); Technical Education and Training (Office of Education); Rehabilitation of Handicapped People (Department of Health, Education, and Welfare); Drug Abuse Information (Departments of Health, Education, and Welfare, Justice,and Defense); Jobs for Veterans (Departments of Commerce, Labor, and Defense); Productivity (National Commission on Productivity); ACTION; U.S. Savings Bonds (Department of the Treasury); Minority Business Enterprise (Department of Commerce); and Food, Nutrition, and Health (Departments of Agriculture and Health, Education, and Welfare).[34]

The advertising agency responsible for the Food, Nutrition, and Health campaign is Young and Rubicam, which also handles the General Foods account. The agency is unlikely to develop a vigorous campaign warning against the nonnutritious products manufactured by General Foods. There may even be a question of conflict of interest. Yet it is common for the Council to assign a public service campaign to an agency that handles a commercial account in the same field. The Council explains that this is because the agency already has the necessary expertise and needs to do no further research. Be that as it may, this practice appears to be another way in which any idea even faintly threatening to the interest of the Council's supporters is excluded.

The Council's endeavors on behalf of the government can be criticized for other reasons. Of the ten campaigns listed, five (Technical Education and Training, Minority Business Enterprise, Rehabilitation, Jobs for Veterans, and Productivity), as well as being intended to improve the economic situation of individuals, are directly concerned with improving the state of the U.S. economy as a whole. The Minority Business Enterprise campaign has as its goal "to increase the participation of minorities in the free enterprise system of the United States."[35] One caustic observer charged that the program is "little more than a charade that finances big business subsidiaries that serve as decoys to industry's often discriminatory hiring and promotion practices."

The most blatant example of a business-oriented campaign is that sponsored by the National Commission on Productivity. According to one participant, it is intended to raise "the overall awareness of individual Americans of the need to increase productivity," and its problem is that "the American people as a whole have no conception of what productivity is all about." Productivity is a "dirty word" that most people equate with "speeding up the production line." The National Commission on Productivity has devised a four-phase program to overcome what it views as the natural antipathy of Americans to the concept of productivity. The first phase avoids any mention of productivity, but speaks of pride in work. After the first slogan idea—"America Didn't Get Great by Goofing Off"—was rejected as too insulting, the slogan "How Would You Like to Sign the Work You Do?" was chosen. This was referred to as "trying to swing in through the back door." The second phase explains what productivity means to the country. In the third phase, the advertisements discuss productivity in relation to the individual. They point out that since most Americans work for only one-third of their lives, they have to be more productive during those years if they want the things Americans have been led to believe everybody should have. The fourth phase discusses the economic future of the United States in relation to the rest of the world. The campaign as a whole is designed to "change the thought of an entire nation."

The other 15 campaigns of the Council, for nonprofit organizations, were: Help Fight Pollution (Keep America Beautiful); Religion in American Life; Aid to Higher Education (Council for Financial Aid to Education); Population (Planned Parenthood); Traffic Safety (National Safety Council); American Red Cross; United Negro College Fund; Register and Vote 1972 (League of Women Voters Education Fund); Consumer Information (Council of Better Business Bureaus); Voluntary Action (National Center for Voluntary Action); Small Claims Courts (Small Claims Study Group); United Way Campaign; Employer

Support of the Guard and Reserve; National Alliance of Businessmen (JOBS program); and VD Awareness (American Social Health Association).[36]

The Better Business Bureau and National Alliance of Businessmen campaigns, while having other goals, also support business interests. Consumer Information can be construed as a public relations pitch for business, as well as an effort to aid consumers, suggesting, as it does, that business is well able to regulate its own. The National Alliance of Businessmen program, aside from helping young people by making them employable, also expands the available labor pool.

Some campaigns, such as Productivity, seem to serve business interests directly, but others work through indirection and by deflecting criticism. For instance, the National Safety Council urges viewers to buckle their seat belts to avoid injury. This reminds the viewer of the safety feature his automobile does have and implies that injuries are caused more by the failure of the individual to buckle up than by the fact that automobiles can be virtual death traps. The energy conservation campaign also works in this manner by informing viewers that they can help alleviate the energy crisis by driving more slowly, turning off lights, and so on. In this way, it is intimated that the crisis is the responsibility of, and can be solved by, the consumer—even though individuals use only 25 percent of the energy, compared to industry's 75 percent.

Consider the Keep America Beautiful campaign. The Council bulletin describes the campaign as follows: "The Ad Council and Keep America Beautiful, Inc., believe that everyone should be environment-conscious and develop an active sense of responsibility for the preservation of a healthy environment. Pollution results from the actions of people and people can put a stop to it."[37] A Keep America Beautiful official emphasized that "the whole campaign is directed toward the individual. We wish generally to stimulate a sense of individual responsibility for environmental improvement. This is a more positive approach than pollution control."

Keep America Beautiful is solely privately funded, with Pepsi Cola a major contributor. (Pepsi sponsors a Keep America Beautiful Day each year and produces commercials urging people to clean up their towns by picking up litter. Pepsi reportedly pays for time to broadcast these spots, although one of the monitored stations broadcast and logged one of them as a PSA.) Other contributors are reportedly Philip Morris, Continental Can, Owens Illinois, Ford Motor Company, American Can Company, United States Brewers Association, and the Glass Containers Manufacturers Institute. Keep America Beautiful, Inc., has actively opposed legislation to require the use of returnable beer and soft drink containers, and in 1974 KAB president and former brewing industry executive Roger Powers testified against such a bill in the California State Legislature. Shortly thereafter, the Sierra Club and other environmentalist groups resigned from KAB's citizen advisory council.[38] It appears that some of the companies which have contributed substantially to the pollution in this country have devised a way in which to deflect criticism by emphasizing the extent to which pollution is the responsibility of individuals, not industry. Thus the campaign equates fighting pollution with antilitter and community clean-up projects, rather than with auto-emission controls, smokestack filters, and prohibitions on disposable bottles and cans.

In contrast to Keep America Beautiful, which is one of the Council's major campaigns, the Environmental Protection Agency receives periodic endorsement by the Council, but has never had major campaign status. This is not for lack of effort on the part of EPA. "We would love to work with them and have tried, but environmental pollution and its control is a complex and controversial problem. It's not easy to get all the supporters of the Council to agree as to what should be said to the public," stated an EPA official. When asked for his opinion of Keep America Beautiful and its slogan "People Start Pollution, People Can Stop It," the official stated: "This is not a theme which this agency would ascribe to, but one which the supporters of the Advertising Council would. Most of the pollution we're concerned with wouldn't be attributed to individuals." Yet broadcasters can cite their showing of KAB PSAs as grounds for rejecting less benign PSAs submitted by environmental groups.

It would be foolish to expect the Advertising Council to support the type of campaign EPA seeks. It is highly unlikely that the executive staff would risk antagonizing the very industries which support the Council. But even if the staff were so inclined, the board of directors would probably veto the proposed campaign. Or the advertising agencies might refuse to handle it, for fear of offending their commercial accounts.Or the networks would be disinclined to feature prominently material that threatens the advertisers upon whom they depend for their very existence.

A case in point is the furor that arose over cigarette commercials in 1967. The FCC ruled that these commercials fell under the fairness doctrine and that stations airing cigarette commercials would also have to air anticigarette PSAs. Many groups were involved in producing these spots, such as the American Cancer Society and the Department of Health, Education, and Welfare; but the Advertising Council never supported any of them, because of its rule of nonacceptance of health campaigns. According to one respondent from a group that sought Council support, "In 1967, the Ad Council was playing a cozy and complex game and simply did not take a stand. Sponsors get first consideration. The Ad Council could not attack the very source of its existence. The basic problem with public service advertising is that it is not a public service organization. In a way, it [the Advertising Council] is a protection for them [the advertising businesses]."

RECENT DEVELOPMENTS

There has recently been some criticism of the Council, most of it originating from "public interest" groups which view the Council as a big-business conspiracy attempting to maintain a monopoly of public service advertising.[39] And there are indications that the Council is beginning to feel somewhat threatened. There is an intriguing statement in a recent annual report: "We must merit the fullest support of the media, and must work in such a manner that the Council is an unchallenged body in the area of public service communications."[40] The Council is attempting to promote itself to the general public, something it has not done before. To this end, it has developed a new logo, which "represents the beginning of a new campaign to develop greater public realization that The Advertising Council works in the public interest thanks to the support of media, advertisers and advertising agencies".[41] The Council has developed full-page magazine advertisements bearing the new logo, which present examples of all the Council's campaigns, attempting to show the public that the Council is indeed providing public service. It is also attempting to increase its public recognition by tagging its television spots with the phrase "this message brought to you as a public service by this station and the Advertising Council."[42] The Council is now determined to "earn full public acceptance and unquestioned credibility."[43]

CONCLUSIONS

As should be obvious by now, those involved in the production of Council campaigns come from a very limited segment of American society, all being drawn from the communications, advertising, and business worlds. Nowhere, either in the Council itself, or among the people with whom it works in the communications and advertising industries, can one find representatives of forces seeking to change the structure of the American economy and polity and to alleviate the problems with which the country is beset—not through mere cosmetic treatment of the symptons, but through basic restructuring and reorganization. Rather, the Council exists in a cozy symbiotic relationship with governmental agencies, nonprofit organizations, advertising agencies, the networks, and the businesses that fund it. By working together and maintaining control of a large percentage of the public service advertising in this country, the Council and its associates shut out dissenting forces and protect their own interests.

Each of the participants in the process has much to gain. The members of the Council believe they are truly dealing with societal problems and, at the same time, have well-paying jobs through which they are able to associate with the elite of the society, both in business and government. The advertising agencies benefit in ways which have been enumerated. The networks, which have space to fill and an avowed public service commitment, receive material that will be noncontroversial and nonthreatening to their advertising interests. Government agencies enjoy inexpensive publicity, as do nonprofit organizations. But, as evidenced by the examination of Council campaigns, the businesses that provide the "sole source of support" for the Council have the most to gain.

NOTES

1. Robert P. Keim, president; Gordon C. Kenney, vice-president, Campaigns Administration and Development; Dean H. Fritchen, vice-president, Media Administration and Development; Norma A. Kramer, editor of *Public Service Advertising Bulletin;* and Emily Caperton, information programs manager (Advertising Council, personal interview, February 21, 1974; hereafter referred to as "Advertising Council interview").

2. Telephone interview with Norma A. Kramer, editor of *Public Service Advertising Bulletin* on October 22, 1976.

3. Ibid.

4. Ibid.

5. J. A. R. Pimlott, "Public Service Advertising: The Advertising Council," *Public Opinion Quarterly* 12 (Summer 1948): 209-19.

6. Ibid., pp. 211-13.

7. The Advertising Council, Inc., *Annual Report 1971-72* (handout), p. 2.

8. Ibid.

9. The Advertising Council, Inc., *Annual Report 1972-73*, p. 23. These figures exclude an additional $1.5 million each year for reimbursements for production and distribution of advertising materials to all media.

10. The Advertising Council, Inc., *Annual Report 1971-72,* p.7.

11. Ibid., p.9.

12. Ibid., p. 10.

13. The National Information Bureau is a private, nonprofit organization, headquartered in New York, which provides information on fund-raising philanthropic organizations such as the American Cancer Society. Its purposes are: "1) to maintain sound standards in its field of philanthropy; 2) to aid wise giving through the provision of information and advisory services for contributors." The bureau prepares reports on various kinds of philanthropic agencies which cover "agency origin, purpose, program, leadership finances, tax deductibility status, and NIB comments and conclusions." The report also judges whether the organization meets NIB standards, which are as follows:

1. Board–An active and responsible governing body, serving without compensation, holding regular meetings, and with effective administrative control.
2. Purpose–A legitimate purpose with no avoidable duplication of the work of other sound organizations.
3. Program–Reasonable efficiency in program management, and reasonable adequacy of resources, both material and personnel.
4. Cooperation–Evidence of consultation and cooperation with established agencies in the same or related fields.
5. Ethical Promotion–Ethical methods of publicity, promotion and solicitation of funds.
6. Fund-Raising Practice–In fund raising:
   a) No payment of commissions for fund raising.
   b) No mailing of unordered tickets or merchandise with a request for money in return.
   c) No general telephone solicitation of the public.

7. Audit–Annual audit, preferably employing the Uniform Accounting Standards and prepared by an independent certified public accountant, showing all Support/Revenue and Expenditures, in reasonable detail. New organizations should provide an independent certified public accountant's statement that a proper financial system has been installed.
8. Budget–Detailed annual budget, translating program plans into financial terms.

All information obtained from the National Information Bureau, *Annual Report, 1973* (handout), pp. 1,4,6. The Advertising Council is a contributing member of the NIB and, as such, is entitled to receive reports on the organizations seeking its support.

14. The Advertising Council, Inc., *The Advertising Council Criteria* (handout, December 1973).

15. Advertising Council interview.

16. Ibid.

17. Ibid.

18. The Advertising Council, Inc., *Annual Report, 1971-72,* p. 10.

19. The Advertising Council, Inc., *Annual Report, 1972-73,* p. 5.

20. Advertising Council interview.

21. A group calling itself POW-MIA Families for Immediate Release challenged the campaign under the fairness doctrine, asserting that the Council was seeking to divert attention from the goal of ending the war in Vietnam. Assertedly as a result of this threat, the campaign failed to gain much air play. See Tom Asher, "Smokey the Bear and the Ad Council," *More*, March 1972, pp. 1-5.

22. The Advertising Council, Inc., *Annual Report 1972-73*, p. 6.

23. Rhatican, who acted as liaison from 1971 to January 1974, left the White House to become vice-president of communications for the American Paper Institute. His Successor was Kenneth W. Clawson, then deputy director of communications for the executive branch. (The Advertising Council, Inc., *Public Service Advertising Bulletin,* January/February 1974, p. 12.)

24. Advertising Council interview.

25. Pimlott, "Public Service Advertising," p. 211.

26. Ibid., p.213. It no longer exists.

27. "Ad Council Reviews Its Priorities," *Broadcasting* 78 (June 22, 1970): 76-78.

28. The announcement, or perhaps more accurately claim, was made by William O'Shaughnessy, president of the New York State Broadcasters Association. See "Energy-Saving Tips to Be Broadcast," New York *Times,* January 6, 1973.

29. "Inaugural Ads: Decisions on Whether to Run," Washington *Post*, January 5, 1973.

30. Ibid.

31. When we were conducting our research the list was as follows:

N.W. Ayer and Son, Inc.
Leo Burnett Company Inc.
Campbell-Ewald Company
Compton Advertising, Inc.
Dancer Fitzgerald Sample, Inc.
D'Arcy-MacManus and Masius, Inc.
Deutsch, Shea and Evans, Inc.
DKG Inc.
Doyle Dane Bernbach Inc.
Foote, Cone and Belding Advertising, Inc.
Grey Advertising Inc.
The Griswold-Eshleman Company
Hutchins/Darcy Inc.
Kenyon and Eckhardt Advertising, Inc.
Lieberman Harrison, Inc.

Liller Neal Battle and Lindsey, Inc.
Richard K. Manoff Advertising, Inc.
Marsteller Inc.
McCaffrey and McCall, Inc.
McCann-Erickson, Inc.
Needham, Harper and Steers Advertising, Inc.
Ogilvy and Mather Inc.
Ross Roy, Inc.
SSC&B, Inc.
Tatham-Laird and Kudner
J. Walter Thompson Company
Vansant, Dugdale and Co., Inc.
Warwick, Welsh and Miller, Inc.
Young and Rubicam International Inc.

(The Advertising Council, Inc., *Annual Report 1972-73,* p. 24.) The Council has now adopted the policy of permitting an agency to handle only one account at a time.

32. Ed Morse, "Pro Bono Publico," Young and Rubicam Advertising Agency (handout), p. 60.

33. The Advertising Council, Inc., *Annual Report, 1972-73,* p. 8.

34. Ibid., pp. 9-16.

35. Ibid., p. 10.

36. Ibid., pp. 9-16.

37. The Advertising Council, Inc., *Public Service Advertising Bulletin,* September/October, 1973, p. 4.

38. Bruce Howard, "The Advertising Council: Selling Lies," *Ramparts* 13 (December 1974-January 1975): 30.

39. See especially ibid., and Asher, "Smokey the Bear," pp. 1-6; Ava Swartz, "Ads for Outgroups," *Columbia Journalism Review* 12 (March-April 1974): 12-15; and "Some Final Flak at AAAA," *Broadcasting* 82 (March 27, 1972): 28.

40. The Advertising Council, Inc., *Annual Report 1972-73,* pp. 2-3.

41. The Advertising Council, Inc., *Public Service Advertising Bulletin,* September/October 1973, p. 2.

42. Advertising Council interview.

43. The Advertising Council, Inc., *Annual Report 1972-73,* p.3.

CHAPTER

3

NON-ADVERTISING COUNCIL CAMPAIGNS

The Advertising Council receives a large percentage of the space available for television public service advertising, but, contrary to the assertions of some public interest groups, it does not maintain a monopoly. Rather, several nationally based organizations successfully vie with the Council for public service time, as do agencies or departments of the federal government which do not receive Council support. How do these organizations, both government and private, go about producing and distributing their spots, what are they attempting to convey to the public, and how do they know whether they are successful in persuading broadcasters to air their material? The key issue here is the obstacles these organizations encounter by not being part of the Advertising Council-advertising agency-broadcaster nexus. This chapter will discuss the public service campaigns of the federal government and of nationally based nonprofit organizations.

GOVERNMENT PUBLIC SERVICE CAMPAIGNS

There are three reasons why a government department might choose not to work with the Council, even if the option were available. First, an Advertising Council campaign can entail an expenditure on the part of the sponsoring agency of anywhere from \$75,000 to \$150,000 in out-of-pocket costs for the production of material. Some agencies believe that they can execute a campaign for less. Second, many agencies wish their campaigns to be directed at a specific or "target" audience. The Advertising Council, according to its criteria, will handle only projects of national concern. Third, the agency may be aware that the Council would not be favorably disposed towards its proposed campaign because of possible conflicts with the interests of the Council and its members. Thus, the Department of Health, Education, and Welfare knew that it was fruitless to request Council support for its antismoking program.

Ten-, thirty-, and sixty-second television spots compose a large percentage of the audiovisual output of the government. The leading sources are the United States Information Agency; the Environmental Protection Agency; the Veterans Administration; and the Departments of Agriculture, Transportation, Treasury, Interior, Defense, and Health, Education, and Welfare.[1] In fiscal 1972, they created 251 such spots at a cost of roughly $1.9 million, an average expenditure of approximately $7,570 per spot.[2] Thus, a government agency that wishes to conduct a public service campaign solely on television may produce one to three spots at a considerable saving over the money required for an Advertising Council multimedia campaign. The Department of Defense accounted for the largest group of these spots, 104, and the greatest expenditure of funds, $556,112.[3]

Most federal government agencies have a division that is solely responsible for producing and distributing audiovisual material concerning its activities. Many possess in-house facilities for the production of the spots, while others contract out the work to production houses of advertising agencies. There has recently been some dispute over the subject of in-house versus outside contract production, and the Office of Management and Budget has directed that there be a policy of "maximum reliance on the private sector for goods and services."[4] At the White House we were told that the government should not be in the business of producing television spots since private production houses can usually be expected to do a better job.

A department which has decided to contract out the development of its campaign follows an established procedure. First the department develops a scope-of-work statement, which includes information on the projected number of PSAs, the topic, the intended audience, and the length. A notice is placed in *Commerce Business Daily* issuing a request for proposals. Production houses and advertising agencies submit both creative and cost proposals. The department narrows the field by selecting companies that present acceptable creative proposals. The department then conducts personal interviews and visits the companies in question to inspect their facilities. It also considers the companies' experience in the public service field and their success in persuading broadcasters to air PSAs.

Ostensibly, a government agency which contracts with an advertising agency or production house accepts the lowest bid. However, there are indications that the low bid is not the only consideration and that the White House might have some influence on what contracts are awarded to whom.

Prior to the election of Richard Nixon to the presidency, the J. Walter Thompson Agency received $160,000 a year for its one account handling the Marines' recruitment campaign. In 1972, the agency reportedly received $3.5 million in federal contracts.[5] Part of this money came from the Food and Drug Administration in payment for the development of a toy safety campaign at a cost of $137,000.[6] Later the Food and Drug Administration contracted with Thompson for a food and nutrition campaign at a cost of $147,000. Robert

Choate, director of the Council on Children, Media and Merchandising, charged that there was a probable conflict of interest here, since Thompson also had several clients in the food industry.[7] In addition to the two Food and Drug Administration contracts, the Marine Corps increased its payments to $3 million.[8] At the time these contracts were awarded, three former Thompson employees, H.R. Haldeman, Dwight Chapin, and Ronald Zeigler, were in positions of importance at the White House. Thompson representatives denied that there was anything improper about their receiving the contracts and contended that the participation of former employees of the firm in high government posts did not work to their advantage. The agency, when criticized, said that it engages in competition with other agencies, is selected by the usual procedure, and has no unfair advantage.[9]

This raises anew the question of how much influence the White House has on government public service advertising. There is evidence that the president's assistant who makes decisions in regard to the Council also oversees non-Council-related public service advertising in government. For instance, scripts of PSAs for the Internal Revenue Service are occasionally sent to the White House for final approval before being produced. And for the Department of the Treasury as a whole, the White House makes recommendations on "sensitive areas," although its approval is not required.

Yet the White House probably does not have as much influence as it would like to have or could have, or that others think it (or some other central agency) should have. One of the complaints frequently voiced about government public service advertising is that it is terribly inefficient. Many government agencies conduct public service campaigns on similar subjects. "People are doing totally duplicate jobs in different federal agencies," we were told. The man at the White House responsible for liaison with the Advertising Council undertook to correct this situation. He claims to have conducted a major overhaul of the drug abuse program, attempting to substitute a unified and coherent message for the plethora of competing messages which had been emanating from the government. He also considered expanding the Smokey the Bear campaign to encompass all the campaigns conducted by several agencies on the environment. While more than $2 million was being spent in several unrelated envirionmental campaigns, he felt he could devise a far more efficient campaign for $100,000 to $200,000. Similarly, funds are being duplicated in the alcohol abuse campaign as the National Council on Alcohol and Alcohol Abuse, funded by federal money, competes for air time with alcohol spots originated by the Departments of Transportation and Health, Education, and Welfare.

It is not entirely clear that duplication equals inefficiency. It may well be that PSAs on the same general subject address themselves to it in different manners, use different techniques, and propose different solutions. A variety of approaches affords broadcasters a wider range from which to choose and, perhaps, makes it more likely that they will find a PSA which is attractive to them and for which they will be inclined to provide broadcast time. Similarly, a variety of approaches enables the government to appeal to several sectors of the population and thus increases the likelihood that the campaign will have impact on more people.

However, many of the people interviewed expressed dismay over what they believed to be apparently useless and expensive replication of effort and were concerned that they lack the contact with their counterparts in other agencies that might help to avoid the situation. One agency's coordinator of public service activities suggested that perhaps an agency is needed to supervise and coordinate government public service efforts to ensure maximum efficiency. The distinctions between coordination, centralization, and control are narrow, and it is unclear whether such an agency would ameliorate or exacerbate existing problems, or generate new ones.

The federal government currently uses public service advertising extensively, and it becomes important to know exactly what is emanating from the active departments. The picture remains somewhat incomplete, since the government issues no comprehensive report on its public service activities. The following information has been gathered from interviews in several representative departments.

The greatest number of PSAs are produced for the United States Information Agency; the Environmental Protection Agency; the Veterans Administration; and the Departments of Agriculture, Transportation, Treasury, Interior, Defense, and Health, Education, and Welfare. Many of the departments conduct Advertising Council-sponsored campaigns of their own, so the list of government campaigns sponsored by the Council in the previous chapter is a good indication of the type of campaign for which these agencies are responsible. A description of a few of these will give a fair overview of government public service activity conducted outside the Advertising Council's ambit.

Grey Advertising and the Department of Transportation have devised a three-year "public information program" whose goal is to reduce the number of fatal automobile accidents caused by drunk drivers. The first phase of the program was intended to create public awareness of the magnitude of the problem through statistics. The second phase was to intensify this awareness by personalizing the problem. This was done through the highly effective "Janie" spot, which pictures a young woman and her family in an idyllic situation while a song describing her aspirations is sung, presumably by the woman. There is a sudden shift from the lively scene to a still photo of the same scene. An announcer informs us that Janie was killed by a drunk driver. This spot won several awards and is believed to be one of the most creative and effective PSAs devised.[10] In the third phase a new theme has been introduced in an attempt to move people from mere awareness to corrective action. The theme is, "a drunken driver is your problem," and the spots urge viewers to find alternatives to allowing their drunken friends to drive.

The Office of Education, which cooperated with the Advertising Council on the Technical Education Training program, developed with the services of a production house the "Right to Read" campaign, which urges people with reading difficulties to seek help from their local branch of the Office of Education. The campaign consists of five spots intended for different audiences and, it is hoped, contributes to decreasing the rate of functional illiteracy in this country.

A public service campaign is conducted by the Internal Revenue Service each year before the deadline for returns. The IRS claims that it is not attempting to change its public image; it simply wishes to inform people about their rights and obligations under the tax laws. One spot informs the viewers that if they have a question concerning their taxes they should contact the nearest office of the agency. Despite its claims that it is not engaged in public relations, these spots could produce an image of the agency as helpful and understanding, rather than threatening. This would also seem to be the case with the two campaigns described above. The Office of Education and the Department of Transportation, while addressing certain specific issues, are simultaneously depicting themselves as contributing to the solution of societal problems. Most other government public service campaigns convey similar impressions. Thus, while PSAs may explicitly instruct viewers how to deal with a specific problem, they appear implicitly to suggest that the government is beneficent and working to their advantage.[11]

Governmental departments whose campaigns are not sponsored by the Advertising Council have to be concerned with the distribution of their PSAs. These departments face a difficult situation, being in direct competition not only with other sectors of the federal government, but with the Advertising Council, national organizations, local organizations, and state and local governments. Those concerned with government public service activities are, for the most part, well aware of this and thus try to make their material attractive not only to the prospective audience, but to the broadcasters as well.

Those interviewed repeatedly stressed that, given the high degree of competition for PSA space, it was absolutely essential that their spot be of high professional quality. It was assumed that a technically deficient spot would be immediately eliminated by a discriminating station manager with better material at hand. Interviewees also expressed the belief that being entertaining helps ensure that a spot will be played. The spot should be "amusing, novel, different, and interesting," and relevant to local communities. According to one interviewee, the government spots have an inherent advantage because of their sponsorship. Originating with the government, he asserted, gives a PSA "one leg up" in the competition.

The departments have devised distributive tactics which consist of more than merely mailing the ads to the stations. The Department of Health, Education, and Welfare encloses a personal letter from the secretary to the station manager requesting that the PSA be played. Often the spots are sent to regional offices whose personnel are expected to contact local stations. Having someone take the ad to the station and talk to the station manager is supposedly more efficacious than sending it by mail.

The Environmental Protection Agency, in an effort to obtain network time, submits story boards to the continuity boards of the networks before producing the spots. Representatives of a prominent advertising agency that handles an account for one branch of the armed services say they regularly go out to talk to people at local stations. They claim never to engage in pressure tactics in such situations. Rather, it is necessary to "be nice" to the stations because "they only have so much time and ten times that amount of people who want the time. The more you can be sympathetic to them and explain what you are trying to do, the better the chance you have of getting time."

As opposed to the Advertising Council, which regularly compiles statistics concerning the use its material receives, government agencies have only the vaguest notion of whether and when their spots are aired by individual stations. Many stations send invoices to the originator of the PSA, stating how many times and when the PSA was played, and how much this would have cost a commercial advertiser, but they do this haphazardly and there is a feeling that these "usage cards" are a less-than-reliable indicator. Yet the government people are hesitant to ask for full and complete reports, feeling that this might antagonize stations with limited time and resources and make them more likely to use someone else's material.

Many of the interviewees stated that because the heavily watched prime-time space is purchased by commercial advertisers, their PSAs wind up "on a rerun of Batman or on the 2:00 a.m. movie." The media coordinator for one department was sharply critical of the networks for following this practice and not providing enough prime time for drug abuse spots. Another practice often followed is to run a block of several PSAs immediately before a station signs off. Respondents were generally pessimistic about improving this situation, given the commercial constraints on broadcasters, but stated that because they were receiving free time, it was best to be content with the situation.

The army, however, was not resigned to this situation. It was in the process of transition from the draft to an all-volunteer force, which meant that recruitment advertising would be increasingly important. To deal with the problem, the army first attempted to make broadcasters more receptive to its PSAs by upgrading their quality, spending anywhere from $60,000 to $80,000 per spot. When this tactic failed to result in the airing of more of its PSAs, the army developed an experimental, paid advertising campaign, which ran from March to June 1971 and reportedly cost $3.5 million. During this period, army commercials were supposedly receiving an "average of 308 million television impressions per month."[12] The army was pleased with the results of the paid advertising, believing that placing the advertisements on programs which would be viewed by the target audience, 18- to 24-year-old males, had increased enlistments. The army concluded that commercial advertising was preferable to reliance on public service advertising.

Congressional opposition, however, caused the paid advertising experiment to be discontinued,[13] and the army mounted an effort to increase its share of public service time. The first step was a letter sent by then Secretary of the Army Robert F. Froehlke to the presidents of the radio and television networks asking for a five- to tenfold increase in the amount of time given army PSAs. Froehlke suggested that the networks had a responsibility to air army PSAs. "Many also believed that radio and television stations which are licensed by the United States government should provide effective public service time to support essential national programs."[14] The networks publicly "politely declined" to comply with this request.

Failing with the networks, the army turned to local stations. It instructed its civilian aides in each state ("well-placed people with a warm spot in their hearts for the army," we were told) to contact their friends at local stations and request more PSA time for the army. Local recruiters were told to deliver the new PSAs which they received personally to the local station managers. In spite of these efforts, the army received only 2 million impressions per month through free public service time, less than 1 percent of the exposure it received through paid advertising.[15]

The army's case highlights the problems inherent in depending upon public service advertising to promote governmental programs. The spots may be produced at no little expense and never be broadcast; or, if they are constructed for a specific audience, they may be broadcast during programs that the members of the target audience are unlikely to watch; or they may be broadcast when no one except a hardened insomniac is likely to be watching.[16] On the other hand, public service advertising does provide a source, albeit unreliable, of free publicity. Coupled with the lack of alternatives available without the expenditure of a great deal of money, the government is likely to remain in the business of producing and distributing PSAs.

CAMPAIGNS BY NONPROFIT ORGANIZATIONS

In addition to the government, a wide range of well-established and relatively well-funded nonprofit organizations mount national public service campaigns without Advertising Council support. Many of these are health-oriented organizations, such as the American Lung Association and the American Cancer Society, which would be unable to obtain Council support even if they were so inclined. The Council has a policy of not accepting for major campaign status any health-related organization, believing that all such campaigns should be conducted under the auspices of the United Way.

The first decision facing an organization which hopes to create a public service campaign is whether to hire an advertising agency or to create and produce the PSAs itself. Many of those interviewed opted for the latter, for two reasons. The first is a simple matter of cost. Most advertising agencies do not do pro bono work for organizations not sponsored by the Advertising Council, and many organizations are unwilling to spend a large portion of their limited funds for the services of an advertising agency. (This is another basis on which the Council can be criticized. It siphons off all the pro bono activities of the largest agencies, leaving those nonprofit agencies not under Advertising Council auspices to find a smaller, less expensive agency or to do the work themselves.)

Many interviewees gave as a second reason the opinion that they could better convey their message without the intervention of an advertising agency, which is accustomed to handling commercial customers and tends to apply the same methods to public service accounts. Perhaps justifying this view, those interviewed in advertising agencies, while saying that public service accounts allow them more creative freedom, also stated that there is essentially no difference between the techniques they use to market a commercial product and those they use to market an idea in a public service campaign. What is effective in one case is supposedly equally effective in another.

After creating the spots, whether with an agency or by itself, the organizations face the problem of persuading broadcasters to air them. They employ much the same techniques as the government, often sending PSAs to local chapters for distribution. The relations with the networks are more complicated. At one network, for example, a non-Advertising Council PSA is reviewed by a public service committee to ensure that it meets the following criteria before it is considered for airing:

1. The PSA must be sufficiently national in scope to appeal to a national audience.
2. It must appeal to a general audience.
3. The sponsoring organization must be devoted entirely to a public service or charitable cause.
4. The organization cannot promote the sale of commercial products.
5. The PSA must not espouse any controversial, partisan, or sectarian causes.
6. If the PSA is for the solicitation of funds, it must meet standards of the National Information Bureau and the Advertising Council.
7. The PSA must deal affirmatively with a cause and must not attack others.

At another network the formal criteria a non-Advertising Council PSA must meet before it can be considered for broadcast include that it be national in scope, espouse a cause that affects a significant portion of the population, not employ "scare tactics," and not be overly violent. As is the case with Advertising Council criteria, these are clearly subject to varying interpretations depending upon the nature of the group in question. (How they are used to exclude groups will be discussed later.) Networks also look at an organization's credentials and attempt to ensure that it has not misrepresented itself. (One would assume that they rely on National Information Bureau materials.)

Both networks encourage organizations to submit story boards of proposed PSAs to the networks prior to filming the spots. The audiovisual director of one association stated, "The networks ask for the story boards ostensibly to give advice, but actually because they are concerned with the editorial content of the spots. The basic stance of the networks is pretty conservative." Whatever the motivations of the networks, the organizations have little choice but to comply if they wish to receive network time.

The networks do not need to apply these screening techniques to Advertising Council material, being aware that nothing of which they might vehemently disapprove is likely to emanate from that source. In the case of organizations not sponsored by the Advertising Council, the networks must apply their own screening techniques. Through the use of the criteria and reviewing story boards, the networks can ensure that they need accept no socially, commercially, or politically undesirable PSAs.

Having distributed the spots, the organizations have only a vague idea of how much play their PSAs receive. Like government departments, they only intermittently receive usage cards from the stations. And because the costs involved in surveying or monitoring the stations are prohibitive, the organizations must rely on information provided by the stations.

CONCLUSIONS

It is clear that both government and nongovernment organizations unconnected with the Advertising Council face problems their Council counterparts do not. For the most part they do not receive the volunteer services of an advertising agency and thus must either pay an agency or produce the PSAs themselves. As opposed to Council organizations, which have their PSAs sent to stations bearing the Advertising Council imprimatur, they must themselves handle distribution of the material and make efforts to persuade broadcasters to use it. They do not have access to the kinds of statistics the Council does and must rely on sketchy and incomplete information about the play their PSAs receive. And finally, because they must first consider the broadcasters, without whose cooperation no one would see the PSAs, the subjects and approaches they can include in their PSAs are limited.

NOTES

1. U.S., Executive Office of the President, Office of Telecommunications Policy, *Report of the Interagency Audio-Visual Study Group, Audio-Visual Communications in the Federal Government* (mimeograph, January 1974), Appendix G.

2. Ibid.

3. The public service output of the Department of Defense consists of recruitment spots for the four services, aired free of charge by broadcasters and logged as PSAs. The question of whether recruitment spots should indeed be considered as public service was raised during the course of the Vietnam war, when several peace groups asked stations for equal time to respond to these spots. A brief discussion of these cases is included in Chapter 5. (Ibid.)

4. U.S., Office of Management and Budget, circular A-76, referred to, p. 2.

5. Jack Anderson, "White House Tie Booms Ad Agency," Washington *Post,* November 30, 1972.

6. A private production house supposedly claimed it could have produced comparable material at a cost of $55,000 (ibid.).

7. "Choate Questions FDA Contract to J.Walter Thompson," *Public Interest Alert,* November 1, 1973, pp. 4-5.

8. Anderson, "White House."

9. Ibid., and "Choate Questions FDA Contract," p.5.

10. This PSA is subjected to further analysis in Chapter 6.

11. This issue will be dealt with at greater length in Chapter 10.

12. Central All-Volunteer Force Task Force, *Broadening the Recruit Market,* U.S., Office of the Assistant Secretary of Defense, Manpower and Reserve Affairs, Department of Defense, November 1972, p. 2.

13. Ibid., p. 13.

14. "Now Army Wants Free Time," *Broadcasting* 81 (September 27, 1973): 27.

15. Central All-Volunteer Force Task Force, *Broadening the Recruiting Market,* p. 2.

16. Data concerning the time periods when PSAs are most likely to be broadcast are discussed in Chapter 4.

CHAPTER

4

LOCAL STATIONS

The penultimate stage of the funneling process occurs at the local television station. The efforts of the producers of PSAs will be for naught if someone at a local station determines not to air the spots. This chapter discusses the obligations of broadcasters under Federal Communications Commission rules and National Association of Broadcasters' guidelines and establishes a general picture of public service advertising policy at the local level. What legal obligations, if any, does the broadcaster have under Federal Communications Commission regulations? What part does the National Association of Broadcasters play in public service advertising? How many PSAs do stations show, on the average, and when are they likely to appear? How many of the PSAs which they receive do they air? What criteria are used to accept or reject PSAs? These questions will be answered through Federal Communications Commission and National Associations of Broadcasters' documents, interviews with their officials, and the data accumulated from questionnaire responses by 106 stations, approximately 15 percent of the 700 television stations in the country.

FEDERAL COMMUNICATIONS COMMISSION

Since the airwaves are considered public property, a government regulatory agency, the Federal Communications Commission, licenses individuals and corporations to operate on a frequency in a particular location. The license is granted with the condition that the broadcasters operate the station in the public interest, and PSAs may be used partially to fulfill this requirement. The Federal Radio Commission defined the public interest as follows:

> Broadcasting stations are licensed to serve the public, and not for the purpose of furthering the private or selfish interests of

individuals or groups of individuals. The standard of public interest, convenience or necessity means nothing if it does not mean this.[1]

The Federal Communications Commission further elaborated on the public interest responsibility of broadcasters, defining it as the "affirmative responsibility on the part of broadcast licensees to provide a reasonable amount of time for the presentation over their facilities of programs devoted to the discussion and consideration of public issues."[2]

The presence of questions concerning PSAs on the license renewal form suggests that the commission considers these advertisements to be one way in which a broadcaster may serve the public interest. Until recently the form merely asked the broadcaster how many PSAs were aired in an average week over the three years of the previous license period, and how many PSAs the broadcaster intends to air per week in the next three years. However, there are no regulations concerning the type, placement, or number of PSAs a station should broadcast; consistency of the figures is all that concerns the commission. Section 326 of the Federal Communications Act prohibits the commission from using censorship power over programming, and that section has been interpreted to include PSAs. The commission has specifically stated, "Whether to present public service announcements for any specific purpose or on behalf of any particular public or private organization is a matter for determination by the individual licensee."[3]

The commission has, however, stated that if a broadcaster proposes to meet his responsibility for serving the needs of his community solely through the use of announcements, it will "place on the applicant proposing only announcements the burden of establishing the adequacy of his proposal."[4] The FCC's judgment is "founded on the recognition that our society is confronted with many complex problems that cannot be met by the brief comment afforded by announcements."[5]

The FCC license renewal form has recently been changed, and one of the revisions relates to public service advertisements. Rather than merely requesting the number of PSAs broadcast in an average week over the past three years, the commission now requires the applicant to respond to the following questions:

> State (a) the minimum total of public service announcements and (b) the minimum number of public service announcements between 8 a.m.-11 p.m. the applicant proposes to broadcast during a typical week.
>
> Of the total number of public service announcements which the applicant proposes to broadcast during a typical week state (a) the number which he expects will be primarily designed to promote programs, activities or services of organizations or organizational units located in the service area, (b) the number he expects will be primarily designed to promote programs, activities or services of organizations or organizational units located outside of the service

> area and (c) the number which he expects will either not fall readily into either category (a) or (b) and/or will be a combination of both.[6]

This was not, however, the way in which the new question was first formulated. The commission had originally stated the new inquiry as follows:

> State (a) the total number of public service announcements, (b) the number of public service announcements involving local organizations and (c) the number of public service announcements aired between 8 a.m.-11 p.m. during the most recent composite week.[7]

The impetus for more detailed questions on PSAs came from an "examination of composite week logs furnished by renewal applicants [which] suggests that similarities in the total number of PSAs for the week does not necessarily mean similarities in the nature of the PSAs or in the time of day in which they were aired."[8] Given this obvious desire to solicit more information than it had previously, what motive did the commission have for subsequently changing the wording of the new question? The answer seems to be that both the networks and the Advertising Council were disturbed by the commission's emphasis on local PSAs. Members of the Advertising Council reportedly protested the wording during a hearing held by the Office of Management and Budget on the new form. NBC argued that stations should not be required to specify the number of local PSAs broadcast "because it is the substance of the PSA rather than the source that is of consequence."[9] The FCC responded by modifying the national-local dichotomy in the first version of the question. The commission recognized that, while some PSAs are easily classifiable as being designed to benefit either local or national organizations, others are not, and there could be genuine differences of opinion as to their proper categorization.

In fairness to the commission, it might be noted that we encountered this very problem when engaged in content analysis of PSAs. For instance, how is a PSA for a national organization that bears a tag line with the address of a local affiliate to be categorized? The FCC attempted to resolve this problem by saying that "the primary beneficiary of the PSA is determinative as to whether or not the PSA is local rather than the location of either the producer of the announcement or the personality who may appear on the screen."[10]

The commission denied that it was requesting this information because it was attempting to formulate any rules concerning placement or type of PSAs: "It should be re-emphasized, however, that in soliciting information regarding programming of PSAs the Commission has never, and it is not now suggesting that there is a certain number of PSAs that should be aired each week or that a certain percentage of PSAs should be primarily designed to benefit organizations or organizational units in the local service area."[11]

In spite of these protestations, it is reasonable to assume that stations will now be more cognizant of their responsibility to air PSAs originated by local groups. And this is perhaps the reason why both the networks and the Advertising Council reacted negatively to including a straight local-national dichotomy in the license renewal form. The Council, operating solely for the production and distribution of national public service advertising, would have its sphere of operation limited if television stations were reluctant to air its PSAs, preferring instead to broadcast spots produced by groups in their areas. And the networks, which have an interest in the continued existence of the Council because it provides them with material with which to fill unsold commercial time and to boost their public image, would understandably agree with the Council in this matter.

As will be discussed later in the chapter, the data garnered from our questionnaire tend to prove that stations are concerned, when selecting PSAs for broadcast, that they be relevant to the needs of the local community. In addition, interviews with groups which have otherwise had little success in obtaining access to television show that stations are more likely to accept the PSAs produced by these groups if they are delivered to the station by and under the sponsorship of local organizations. The inclusion of a question concerning the number of local PSAs aired on the FCC license renewal form may lead to greater acceptance of local PSAs and, thus, incline stations to be receptive to hitherto excluded groups which manage to obtain local sponsorship for their PSAs.*

NATIONAL ASSOCIATION OF BROADCASTERS

We assumed that the broadcasters' trade association and lobbying organization would have some input into the public service advertising process. Yet the National Association of Broadcasters seems to have little concern for public service advertising. When we tried to obtain information concerning the NAB's role and the impact of PSAs, the director of the code authority replied, "I truly doubt I am qualified to throw much light on the subject. Rather, I think you should seek comments from appropriate participants at the Advertising Council and at networks and stations which have run PSAs and would be better equipped to relay audience reaction known to them, etc."[12] The NAB code authority makes only one reference to PSAs:

> Requests for time for the placement of public service announcements or programs should be carefully reviewed with respect to the

---

*Unfortunately, our questionnaire was conducted before the emergence of this issue and elicited no information concerning the percentage of national PSAs broadcast.

> character and reputation of the group, campaign or organization involved, the public interest content of the message, and the manner of its presentation.[13]

It seems that broadcasters operating under these guidelines would be more likely to accept PSAs produced by the Advertising Council, well-established nonprofit groups, and the government. Given the large quantity of PSAs stations receive,[14] it is obviously easier for the public service director to broadcast the PSAs which he knows will be noncontroversial and of good technical quality, rather than to conduct extensive research into the credentials of little-known, newly formed organizations with which he has no experience.

Until recently, the above guideline was the only reference the NAB made to PSAs. As a result of the anticigarette PSA controversy, however, PSAs were included under the taste and claims substantiation section of the NAB television code. An NAB official indicated that because of their "nature" the NAB might be inclined to give a more "liberal interpretation" of these standards in relation to PSAs. The only instance of consultation with the National Association of Broadcasters we encountered was the case of the American Cancer Society, which was considering a PSA on self-examination for breast cancer. The society wished to depict a woman in her home examining herself. The NAB advised that it would be preferable to show the woman receiving an examination conducted by a woman physician in her office.

The NAB official we interviewed also stated that the NAB does not usually consult with stations concerning the acceptability of PSAs, getting involved on a "trouble-shooting basis. Our involvement in the matter is a drop in the bucket."

LOCAL BROADCASTERS

Within the parameters of these very general FCC and NAB guidelines, the local station broadcaster has discretion to do as he wishes. He may accept or reject PSAs, air as few or as many as he pleases, and schedule them for any time as often as he desires. Previously, few data had been available concerning the bases upon which the public service directors at individual stations made these decisions. This is unfortunate,since the station level constitutes the penultimate stage of the funneling process. It was therefore important to obtain data concerning the policy setting and decision making of public service directors. To this end, we sent an 11-part questionnaire to 177 representative stations throughout the United States. The response rate was 61 percent.

We first sought to elicit the broadcasters' views of the usefulness of public service advertisements in fulfilling their stations' public service responsibilities. PSAs were ranked third. Public affairs and news programs were first and second; instructional and religious programs, fourth and fifth respectively.

The data from this question can be related to the controversy concerning whether issues can be best dealt with in PSAs or in some other format. Broadcasters accused of not airing the PSAs produced by excluded groups often argue that they are giving satisfactory coverage to the issue in question through other formats, notably news and public affairs programs. Although broadcasters assert that they rely on these programs to fulfill their public interest responsibility, rather than on PSAs, because issues can be better handled in these formats, there are other possible explanations. In contrast to news and public affairs programs, spot announcements explicitly try to persuade. Broadcasters may thus be reluctant to deal with what they think are controversial issues through PSAs because of possible adverse effects on their advertisers. Advertisers, because PSAs use similar forms and techniques to their own commercials, may be inclined to view PSAs as direct competition, whereas news and public affairs programs, using different techniques, constitute less of a threat.

Another reason may be that broadcasters have editorial control over the content of news and public affairs programs. The broadcaster can decide what approach the programs should take and what should be included and excluded. With PSAs, the broadcaster can only decide whether or not to provide air time. It is obviously to the broadcasters' advantage to fulfill their obligation to provide coverage of controversial issues through a format over which they have editorial control. (Issues raised in PSAs produced by groups which have their PSAs excluded infrequently appear on television in any form.) Moreover, a PSA because of length and techniques, usually presents only one side of an issue, whereas a news or public affairs program provides an opportunity for an apparently more balanced discussion.

We felt that broadcasters' assessment of PSAs as a method of fulfilling their public interest responsibility should be related to the percentage of commercial time devoted to PSAs, the number broadcast each week, the time periods during which they are broadcast, the criteria used for acceptance or rejection, the percentage of PSAs accepted for airing, and the percentage of those actually aired. In fact, the answers to question 1 were crosstabulated with the answers to questions 2 through 7, and several significant relationships were obtained. The broadcaster who ranked PSAs first also tended to devote a greater percentage of commercial time to them, to show more PSAs, to show more during the morning, to consider the group's reputation the most important criterion for selection, to accept for airing more of the PSAs he received, and to air more of those he accepted. Conversely, the broadcaster who ranked PSAs as being of less importance tended to show fewer of them both in percentage of commercial time and total number, to reject more of the ones sent to him, and to air fewer of those he had on hand.

Questions 2 and 3 sought to determine, on the average, how much time stations devote to PSAs. A majority of all respondents consigned less than 10 percent of their commercial time to PSAs, with 25 percent consigning less than

5 percent. Thus, for the most part, public service advertising constitutes a relatively small percentage of total commercial time, although the absolute number of PSAs is substantial. It is only to be expected that a station which is receiving a lot of paid advertising would air relatively few PSAs, since the data indicate that they are only shown during unsold time spots. The majority of respondents broadcast an average of 51 to 150 PSAs weekly, while showing from 510 to 1500 commercials.* Unfortunately, since PSAs vary in length from 10 to 60 seconds, it is impossible to approximate how much time, in minutes, is devoted by these stations to PSAs. However, a study conducted at the University of Connecticut throws some light on this matter. An analysis of PSAs broadcast by four television stations during 530 hours on the air revealed that 747 minutes, or 12.45 hours, were devoted to the 1159 PSAs, compared with approximately 112 hours devoted to commercials.[15] Expressed differently, PSAs occupy 1 of every 43 minutes of air time.

Question 4 was intended to determine the time periods during which PSAs are most frequently aired. It can be argued that, while the previous stages of the process are important in that they exclude groups and determine the content of those spots which are produced, if the PSAs, once made, are simply aired during the least-viewed time periods, their intended beneficial impact may be diluted. Indeed, almost all of those who have either proposed to study or have studied public service advertising have approached the subject in this limited sense, with the question of time and placement uppermost in their minds. They have been concerned with "how to encourage the professional communicator to promulgate PSA messages during times of maximum exposure, and even more importantly, to broadcast those PSAs to appropriate audiences."[16]

We, too, felt that since broadcasters use PSAs to fill unsold commercial time, most PSAs would appear in hours unattractive to commercial advertisers because of the relatively small audience. This coupled with our own random viewing prior to the project, had led to the belief that most PSAs would be broadcast during the late evening hours. Our data revealed that 91.8 percent of all respondents aired only 0 to 25 percent of their PSAs during prime time, and this supports the hypothesis. Yet PSAs were not heavily concentrated in the late evening, as had been suspected. Rather, most respondents indicated that they were equally distributed among the morning, afternoon, and late evening hours. This contradicts the contentions of the producers of PSAs that their products mainly are aired during the late evening.

---

*This number most probably excludes network PSAs, since our experience with one of the monitored stations, WRDU-TV, an NBC affiliate in Durham, North Carolina, has shown that network PSAs may not be logged by affiliates.

Question 5 sought to establish, according to the broadcasters' perceptions, those qualities of a PSA which would enhance its likelihood of receiving air time; as well as to determine the criteria by which broadcasters judge PSAs. PSA producers had indicated that professional quality is the primary determinant of acceptance. The broadcaster ranked the nature of the subject first, followed by reputation of the sponsoring group, professionalism, relevance to the local community (this was the main entry in the "other" category), and length. An explanation for this divergence between the perception of producers and broadcasters lies in the fact that our interviews were conducted, for the most part, with representatives of well-established groups who have little difficulty in getting their PSAs aired. Since these groups have a national reputation and are dealing with noncontroversial material, they need not be concerned with the broadcasters' first two criteria, but only with that of professionalism.

It is possible, incidentally, that the decisions of some local stations about which public service advertisements to show are influenced by the willingness of the sponsoring agencies to donate money to their state's association of broadcasters. The FCC is apparently of the opinion that contributors in some states receive preferential treatment and that some of the donations are spent by the associations for general expenses. It is considering requiring stations to log and label such PSAs.[17]

It can be seen that broadcasters would likely be disposed to provide time for PSAs of well-established groups whose PSAs are noncontroversial and professionally produced. The application of these criteria would at the same time make it less likely that a newly formed advocate group, espousing a controversial position, with little funds for production of a quality spot, would be able to persuade broadcasters to air its PSAs. This is mainly because of the flexibility of the first criterion, the nature of the subject matter. We purposely did not define the meaning of this phrase, wishing to leave it to the broadcaster's interpretation. But, it can be concluded that the use of this criterion results in enormous discretion for the person applying it in the selection of PSAs. This, in turn, most probably results in the exclusion of controversial PSAs because most decision makers would not be long employed at most television stations were they inclined to support and advocate controversial views.

Given a limited amount of time available for airing of PSAs, it is likely that some of the PSAs a station receives will be immediately discarded through application of the criteria listed. Thus, question 6 asked the broadcaster to indicate what percentage of PSAs received was accepted for airing, and question 7 asked him to indicate what percentage of those accepted is actually aired. Most respondents accept no more than 75 percent of the PSAs they receive; they reject or discard the remainder.

These figures indicate that the local station level is indeed a highly important part of the funneling process. A surprisingly large percentage of the groups that pass through all previous stages of the process will never have their PSAs broadcast. And from information which will be discussed in the next chapter, it would seem that the PSAs rejected for broadcast include virtually all the products of small, newly formed advocate groups dealing with controversial issues.

It is useful to compare our data with the results of a survey conducted by the National Public Relations Council during September 1973. The NPRC was interested in ascertaining the treatment accorded PSAs produced by health-related organizations. The survey was sent to 180 public service directors at the networks affiliates in the 60 largest cities in the country. (The response rate is not indicated.) They found that many stations reject as many as 50 percent of the PSAs they receive from national organizations. On the average, according to the results of this survey, 25 percent of all PSAs received are never aired. This figure corresponds with ours. More than half the stations indicated that they broadcast more local than national PSAs and would broadcast even more if they were available. The public service directors felt that the American Cancer Society, ACTION, and the Department of Health, Education, and Welfare produce the best PSAs, with the United Way and the American Lung Association often mentioned.[18]

Our questions 8 and 9 provide a rough measure of the extent to which stations are willing to cooperate with local groups. It was felt that a local group that wishes to follow a televised PSA with further information provided through the mail might request the aid of the local station. Question 8 inquired as to whether any of the PSAs aired by a broadcaster asked the viewer to contact the station for further information. Question 9 asked for the approximate degree of public response elicited by these PSAs. Twenty-four percent of all respondents indicated that they broadcast such PSAs and that a majority of these received at least some requests for further information. The data indicate that most stations do not provide local groups with this kind of assistance, but that if they do, they can expect to receive a response from the local community.

This gives a general description of the public service advertising policy of a majority of our respondents.[19] The data from the questionnaire can also be used to draw inferences concerning the effects of network affiliation. We hypothesized that network affiliates would show fewer PSAs than independent stations because affiliates air more popular programming, which is likely to attract larger audiences than the diet of syndicated reruns and old movies prevalent on independents. Advertisers would therefore be more likely to purchase time on network affiliates, leaving less time for PSAs. Surprisingly, however, network affiliates tended to devote a higher percentage of commercial time to PSAs than did independent stations. But our suspicion was confirmed that because of the high commercial value of prime-time advertising space networks would show very few PSAs in prime time and their affiliates would follow this pattern. Independent stations tended to air more PSAs in prime time and fewer in the morning, as compared with network affiliates. Insofar as criteria of selection are concerned, network affiliates on the average were more concerned with the reputation of the sponsoring group, while independents were inclined to rely more on the professional quality of the spots.

The network-independent distinction was the only variable significantly related to differences in station response. We had felt that the size of the market, the geographic location of the station, and the frequency on which it broadcast (UHF or VHF) would also produce significant differences. They did not. The most important distinction between the public service policies of individual stations lies in the decision making of the public service director, who is responsible for the differences between what is aired on his station and what is aired on the other stations.

Corroborating this conclusion are data we obtained by comparing the PSAs broadcast during the week of April 21, 1973, over two stations: WRDU-TV, a UHF, NBC affiliate located in Durham, North Carolina, and WDCA-TV, a UHF independent station located in Washington, D.C. (more about this in Chapter 7). During the monitored week, WRDU and WDCA broadcast only two of the same PSAs, a Red Cross "Alice" spot and a National Wildlife Federation ad. When we interviewed them, both public service directors indicated they were disposed to air environmental PSAs. There were five broadcast by the Durham station and six in Washington, but, aside from the National Wildlife Federation ad, they were sponsored by different organizations. The director in Durham, an ex-navy man, said he liked to air military recruitment PSAs. We recorded four at his station, three of which were for the navy. The director of WDCA in Washington, D.C. , a woman, expressed a dislike for the military. There were no military PSAs shown on her station.

Our evidence all points to the importance of station gatekeepers in the funneling process. Being little influenced by Federal Communications Commission rules, National Association of Broadcasters guidelines, or the frequency or location of their stations, they use flexible criteria and personal preference to make the decision as to whether a PSA will reach the public.

NOTES

1. 3 FRC, *Annual Report*, "Great Lakes Broadcasting Co.," 1929, p. 32.

2. 13 FCC, *Reports*, "On Editorializing," 1970, p. 1249.

3. U.S., Federal Communications Commission, *The FCC and Broadcasting*, January 15, 1974, sec. 6(a), " Acceptance, Rejection, Scheduling, Cancellation and Duplication of Program Matter; Entertainment Format Changes; Color and Stereo Broadcasting; Adherence to Published Program Schedules" (handout), p.6.

4. 36 *Fed. Reg.* 4102 (1971).

5. Ibid. The issue of the relative merits of dealing with important issues through public service announcements versus other formats such as news programs will be discussed in Chapter 5.

6. 43 FCC 2nd., *Report*, "Broadcast License Renewals" (1975), p. 86.

7. Ibid., p. 38.

8. 27 RR 2d (1973), p. 619.

9. Ibid.

10. Ibid., p. 642a. Category (c) was devised to subsume those PSAs falling clearly under neither (a) nor (b).

11. Ibid.

12. Letter from Stockton Helffrich, director, Code Authority, National Association of Broadcasters, to David L. Paletz, February 14, 1974.

13. National Association of Broadcasters, "Program Standards," *The Television Code Authority*, 17th ed. (April 1973), sec. II, par. 2, p. 3.

14. The research done by the Council on Children, Media and Merchandising indicates that small stations may receive as many as 20 PSAs per week. See Robert B. Choate, "Correcting a Public Disservice: Broadcaster Abuse of Public Service Announcements," mimeographed (Washington, D.C., 1973), p.5. The former public service director at WRDU-TV, an NBC affiliate in Durham, North Carolina, stated that he received, on the average, three PSAs per day.

15. Gerhard J. Hanneman et al., "An Analysis of Televised Public Service Advertising," Drug Abuse Information Research Project, no. 9 (Storrs: University of Connecticut, June 1972), p. 7. Thus, the commercial time devoted to PSAs by these four Hartford stations, agrees with the answers given by our questionnaire respondents.

16. Ibid., p. 19.

17. "Extend Waiver Axe on PS Ads to July," *Variety*, February 19, 1975.

18. National Public Relations Council, "Outstanding TV Spots for 1973," *Channels* 26, no. 5 (November 1, 1973): 1-2.

19. Questions 10 and 11 sought to elicit broadcasters' experiences with the impact of particular PSAs and are discussed in Chapter 6.

CHAPTER

5

THE EXCLUDED

The previous chapters have dealt with the stages of the funneling process, tracing public service campaigns from their inception to their eventual airing on the networks or by local stations. This chapter deals with groups excluded at one level or another of the process. The purpose is to pinpoint the variables which make it difficult for certain groups to reach the public through public service advertising. There will be a general discussion of these exclusionary variables, followed by illustrative case studies.

Many advocate groups never consider public service advertising as a possible way to further their goals. They may believe that other avenues are available to them. For instance, a representative of the American Civil Liberties Union in Washington, D.C., asserted that the organization receives all the publicity it needs through the news media and that advertising would merely be superfluous.

A group may look upon public service advertising as being an inappropriate forum for the presentation of its arguments. As will be discussed later, a case can be made for the position that 30- or 60-second television spots are sometimes not the best way to present a discussion of serious issues.

A group may think it would be in its interests to engage in public service advertising, but be unaware of the procedures to follow. For example, when representatives of the gay liberation movement met with executives of the NBC television network to make complaints and express demands, one of their demands was for public service announcements to counteract antigay prejudice. They were apparently told that PSAs are "approved by stations which should be contacted."[1] This disingenuous response no doubt provided the first in a series of obstacles that the gays and any minority group representing a position threatening to the sociocultural consensus have to face if they want to use PSAs to present, let alone advance, their positions. Thus, when KNBC, the NBC-owned and operated affiliate in Los Angeles, agreed to show PSAs for gays, the commercials were for the Gay Community Service Center, a nonprofit social welfare agency offering free services to gay men and women.[2] No advocacy or endorsement of gay behavior was permitted.

Compounding their problems, small, newly formed advocate groups do not have the strong ties to the advertising and communications businesses that older, better-established, more respectable organizations enjoy. They usually do not know how to obtain the services of an advertising agency or production house, are not familiar with the techniques required for in-house production, and have no methods to ensure that their spots will be aired if they do discover how to produce them.

A group may overcome these obstacles only to discover that the production of television spots is a costly business; an average PSA costs anywhere from $5,000 to $12,000 to produce. And not only does a spot have to be made, it must be reproduced, which also involves major expenditures.

Even if a group has both the necessary expertise and the necessary funds, it is usually unable to compete on the same level with the larger and more expensive advertising agencies and production houses used by the Advertising Council, the government, and well-funded nonprofit organizations. Thus, it produces relatively unprofessional material which station personnel eliminate on this basis, often without even considering the nature of the announcement.

It is only when a group has overcome all these obstacles that it may be excluded because of the content of its PSAs. It should, of course, be noted that lack of expertise and resources may be causally related to a group's controversial status. Groups which espouse views and values upon which there is general consensus in the society, and which are not threatening to advertising or business interests, often find it easier to obtain the resources and expertise necessary to produce PSAs and have them broadcast. These noncontroversial groups are able to enter and to become a part of the network of relationships previously described among the Advertising Council, advertising agencies, broadcasters, nonprofit organizations, the White House, and government agencies. The groups with which this chapter is concerned are unable to do so, for a number of reasons.

THE ADVERTISING COUNCIL AND CONTROVERSIAL GROUPS

The Advertising Council has been notoriously unreceptive to groups whose ideas either threaten business interests or provoke controversy in the society. The Council uses a variety of methods to forestall the efforts of these groups to obtain its support. The first exclusionary variable is intangible. Many advocate groups understand the nature of the Council and are well aware that endeavoring to acquire its backing would be a waste of time and energy. It is impossible to provide quantitative evidence in support of this assertion, but many representatives of excluded groups indicated that this was the case for their organizations.

A major exclusionary factor vis à vis the Council is purely economic. The Council asserts that in return for an outlay of $75,000 to $150,000 in out-of-pocket costs, a group will receive many times that amount in free advertising. In terms of the advertising world and of the budgets of government and well-established nonprofit organizations this may be a modest expenditure. But for most newly formed and struggling advocate groups, this sum represents a major part of the budget which might better be spent in more direct pursuit of their goals than in advertising.

The Council can use many methods to frustrate the efforts of groups seeking its approval. Since the Advertising Council relies on National Information Bureau evaluations, a group must first meet the standards of the NIB. This was apparently one of the problems encountered by an organization called American Freedom from Hunger in its extensive dealings with the Council. Freedom from Hunger raises money for overseas development programs in countries which have been stricken by drought, famine, and other natural disasters. Reportedly it is not looked upon with favor by many in powerful positions because of the politics of food distribution. Whereas an organization such as CARE is willing to cooperate with the Agency for International Development, Freedom from Hunger refuses to do so. This is apparently one reason why the National Information Bureau withheld approval of the organization. The formal justification was that Freedom from Hunger does not use proper auditing procedures in its Hunger Marches. (These are walks in which teen-agers participate and people pledge a certain amount for each mile walked.) Freedom from Hunger's response is that because of the age of the participants it is ridiculous to request audits.

Another of the tactics the Council can employ is to force a group to endure a great many bureaucratic procedures before either assenting to or denying a request for support. This was the experience of Public Communications, Inc., a group engaged mainly in counteradvertising. PCI endeavored to get Advertising Council support for a number of spots dealing with consumerism. The Council never refused, but constantly required clarifications necessitating considerable research. Similarly, when Freedom from Hunger approached the Council with an idea for a coordinated campaign with CARE and similar agencies to raise funds to alleviate a famine in Africa, the Council made so many requests and specifications that "you'd have to set up a Department of Agriculture to do what they wanted."

The seven criteria of the Council are often used to deny a group's requests. For instance, a group called Joint Action in Community Service, which has established a network of volunteers to find employment for members of the Job Corps, was told that it was ineligible for support under Council criteria. Why it should be eliminated while the National Alliance of Businessmen was accorded major campaign status is questionable.

As was mentioned, the Council's criteria do not seem to be the sole factor determining approval. In spite of its assertions, it is likely that the Council is concerned that the group not be opposed to business interests. This is probably the reason for the problems encountered by Public Communications, Inc.

Some of our respondents also asserted that the Council considered the political status of a group, being especially concerned that it be acceptable to the current presidential administration. Freedom from Hunger had reportedly antagonized the Nixon administration because one of its members had, at an international conference, made a statement critical of Nixon's conduct of the Vietnam war. In addition, the majority of the members of the group's board of directors are Democrats, with some even on the White House "enemies list." Sources within the organization believed that if Senator George McGovern had won the 1972 election, Freedom from Hunger would not have had trouble in obtaining the full support of the Council.

The Advertising Council is not, of course, the only route of access to network and station public service time. However, the Council's endorsement makes the task of seeking access much easier, so many excluded groups seek at least to be included in the Council bulletin. Yet many groups never bother to contact the Council, either because they realize that the Council would not be receptive, because they lack the requisite funds, or perhaps because they are concerned that Council acceptance would weaken their intended message. For example, we learned from several sources that Planned Parenthood, whose campaign the Council finally accepted after lengthy negotiations, was forced to make its message less controversial. Originally planning hard-hitting spots, the eventual slogan used was the relatively innocuous "Children by Choice, Not Chance." The whole issue of abortion, in which the group is involved, was totally avoided. Similarly, a group may present its message in a less controversial manner when approaching the Council for support. This was the case with Public Communications, Inc., and its consumerism spots.

LOCAL STATIONS

Because of the same factors—lack of resources, expertise, and contacts in the communications and advertising worlds, and the controversial nature of their PSAs—these groups usually meet with little success when they turn to local stations. For instance, after failing with the Council, both Public Communications, Inc., and Freedom from Hunger distributed to local stations the spots they had produced. In the case of Public Communications, Inc., the majority of the stations gave the spots little play because they considered them too controversial.[3] The Freedom from Hunger spots were not played by any of the stations to which they were sent. Zero Population Growth, although it lacked both funds and a staff member acquainted with the media, produced two series of television spots concerning population control. The group felt that without Advertising Council support it was fruitless to approach the networks and, instead, sent the spots to local chapters for distribution, managing in this way to have the spots played a few times.

THE COUNCIL ON CHILDREN, MEDIA AND MERCHANDISING

The experiences of the Council on Children, Media and Merchandising best elucidate those factors which operate to exclude a group which has overcome the initial obstacles involved in a public service campaign. This group, in concert with the Society for Nutrition Education and the National Council of Negro Women, produced in the fall of 1972 three nutrition education and dental health PSAs intended for broadcast during children's programs. One 30-second cartoon depicted the consequences of overeating snack food, a 60-second puppet sequence dealt with the relationship between sugar and dental problems, and a 60-second live-action sequence discussed the hidden volume of sugar in many foods. The spots appear to be of high professional quality. In contrast to the Advertising Council campaign produced by Young and Rubicam and sponsored by the Departments of Agriculture and HEW, and the Grocery Manufacturers of America, however, the Council on Children, Media and Merchandising's spots strongly attack the advertising-inspired American predilection for non-nutritive foods and snacks high in sugar content. For a year and a half, the Council on Children, Media and Merchandising strove to persuade the networks and local stations across the country to air the spots. The PSAs were sent to all the networks and to 70 stations whose licenses were up for renewal. It was felt that these stations would react most favorably, wishing to prove to the Federal Communications Commission that they were indeed operating in the public interest, convenience, and necessity. Letters accompanied the spots, explaining that they could "bring about a clearer understanding of food values and concerns than now exists on the air."[4] The stations were urged to broadcast the spots "twice each Saturday morning after 8:30 a.m., and once each weekday afternoon between 4:30 p.m. and 6:30 p.m. over the next thirteen weeks."[5]

All three networks flatly refused to air the PSAs. It is worthwhile to examine some of their reasons in the light of our previous discussion of network public service policy. NBC complained that the announcements "take a negative approach. A better approach would appear to be one which affirmatively presents the need for balanced diets."[6] This reflects the NBC criterion that PSAs must deal affirmatively with a cause and must not attack others. By excluding groups such as the Council on Children, Media and Merchandising, which do not meet this standard, NBC is able to prevent any attacks on its advertisers, in this case, the food manufacturers. In response to the assertion of Robert Choate, head of the Council on Children, Media and Merchandising, that the food commercials the networks air constitute food advice to young viewers, the CBS position was: "Since, however, we do not view commercials as 'food advice' urging a steady diet of the advertised products, we do not view nutrition and health broadcasts as necessary to balance or compensate for what you assert is television's 'nutritionally unbalanced' menu."[7] This would seem to be an attempt on the part of the legal department of the network to negate any fairness doctrine considerations of food advertising. CBS also pointed out that it has aired nutrition spots prepared by such groups as the American Dental Association, the American Medical Association, and the National Dairy Council. One need not speculate as to why the PSAs produced by these groups are welcome to the networks while the Choate spots were anathema. In addition, CBS indicated it was interested in using the PSAs of the Advertising Council's new nutrition campaign.[8] ABC stated that although the spots are attractively produced, each raises "sufficient question as to accuracy, controversy or taste as to render it unacceptable for airing as a public service announcement."[9] These might appear to be valid objections, but they also enabled the networks to reject spots that were threatening to the interests of food manufacturers, whose advertising provides a part of the networks' revenue.

The 70 local stations reacted similarly, although there were fewer point-blank refusals. Indeed, 38 stations agreed to air the spots, and 28 declined to do so. Four never replied to Choate's letter. However, persuading those 38 stations to cooperate required a great deal of effort on the part of the Council on Children, Media and Merchandising. Stations which did not reply to the first letter were sent several follow-up letters, the last containing quotes from the station's license renewal form of the station's assertions that it was truly operating in the public interest. A carbon copy of this letter was sent to the chief of the FCC license renewal division. As we explained in the previous chapter, however, no legal pressure could be brought to bear. The Choate organization hoped that the threat of accusing the stations of a violation of the fairness doctrine when their licenses were up for renewal would make them more likely to air the spots. When the stations received this last letter, the Council began receiving calls from station lawyers and "nasty letters" from station managers. Apparently the stations were indeed beginning to feel threatened.

The reasons the stations gave for their refusal indicate where the power lies in public service advertising. An NBC affiliate, WRC in Washington, D.C., refused because NBC had turned down the spots and WRC-TV, as an NBC-owned station, abides by the same standards. Many stations inquired as to whether the spots had the approval of the Advertising Council. A New Orleans station replied: "As a result of a check of the current major PSA campaigns approved by the Advertising Council as well as other local commitments, and without attempting to judge the merits of your position in this matter, we feel that we should not allocate air time for the messages you are sponsoring at this time." Other stations said that they were "swamped with requests" to air PSAs and that since they were already broadcasting nutrition spots by the American

Dental Association, American Medical Association, and so on, they did not believe it necessary to allow time for the Council on Children, Media and Merchandising. These same stations also pointed to regular programs, which they asserted dealt with nutrition. In many instances, the Choate people did not agree that the programs in question adequately dealt with the issues with which they were concerned. Several stations commented that the spots were in questionable taste, dealt with controversial issues, and made unproven assertions concerning the deleterious effects of sugar on health.

A few of the stations indicated that they gave preference to PSAs sponsored by a local group. In the fall of 1973, the Council on Children, Media and Merchandising began to receive letters from consumer groups in all areas of the country asking if they could be of assistance in placing the spots. These groups have reportedly been more successful than the Council, perhaps because stations are indeed more receptive to local groups. Nonetheless, the Council was unable to find out when and how many times its spots were aired by cooperating stations. The stations stated that they had neither the time nor the resources to provide this information, although many of them do compile data for other groups.

The Council on Children, Media and Merchandising was disappointed with the results of its efforts. It spent $5,000 producing the three PSAs and "then it turned into blackmail, trying to get the spots on." It does not plan to engage in public service advertising again because it has now discovered "how closed the airwaves are, and it wouldn't be worth the effort to do it again."

Although the Choate organization did not pursue the possible fairness doctrine implications of broadcasters' refusals to air its PSAs, certain groups attempting to obtain access have used this method with limited success. A brief description of a few of the more important cases will elucidate the role the Federal Communications Commission plays in limiting or obtaining access to the media for groups which are otherwise excluded.

THE FCC AND THE FAIRNESS DOCTRINE

The Federal Communications Commission's first general statement on the fairness doctrine appeared in its 1949 Report on Editorializing by Broadcast Licensees. Simply put, " 'the doctrine imposes two affirmative responsibilities on the broadcaster: coverage of issues of public importance must be adequate and must fairly reflect differing viewpoints.' "[10] But it is the broadcasters' responsibility to make reasonable judgments in good faith on the facts of each situation as to whether a controversial issue of public importance is involved, which viewpoints have been or should be presented, the format and spokesmen to present viewpoints, and all other facets of such programming.

It was not until 1967 that the fairness doctrine was applied to advertising, commercial or public service. In that year, the Federal Communications

Commission declared that cigarette advertising constituted a "controversial issue of public importance" and suggested that a station might "present a number of public service announcements of the American Cancer Society or HEW" [11] to balance its programming. However, the FCC specifically limited the scope of this ruling to cigarette advertising as a "unique situation," stating that the ruling "applies only to cigarette advertising and imposes no fairness doctrine obligation upon petitioners with respect to other product advertising."[12] In response to the ruling, the three networks created special positions for antismoking spots but discontinued this practice when the ban on cigarette advertising on television went into effect on January 2, 1971. As a result, the number of antismoking commercials was then reduced by at least three-quarters.[13]

In March 1970, an environmental group called Friends of the Earth filed a petition against WNBC-TV in New York City, charging the station with failure "to comply with the fairness doctrine or to meet its public interest obligations concerning coverage of the issue of air pollution caused by automobiles and gasoline."[14] Friends of the Earth argued that the cigarette ruling should apply to automobile advertising because both posed a similar threat to health. The Federal Communications Commission ruled against the plaintiffs, saying that the cigarette ruling was not a precedent and that even if it were, "we would not extend the ruling generally to the field of product advertising. . . . Were we to adopt a scheme of announcements tracking in a significant ratio the ordinary product commercials, the result would be the undermining of the present system, based as it is on such commercials."[15] In August 1971, the U.S. Court of Appeals of the District of Columbia overturned the Federal Communications Commission, arguing that the cigarette precedent could not logically be limited to cigarette advertising.[16]

The FCC's latest position is that "an application of the fairness doctrine to normal product commercials would, at best, provide the public with only one side of a public controversy. In the cigarette case, for example, the ads run by the industry did not provide the listening public with any information or arguments relevant to the underlying issue of smoking and health."[17] The precedent of requiring responses to cigarette advertisements is now referred to as "not at all in keeping with the basic purposes of the fairness doctrine."[18] The FCC majority continues: "If in the future we are confronted with a case similar to that presented by the cigarette controversy, it may be more appropriate to refer the matter to Congress for resolution."[19] It concludes, "In the future, we will apply the fairness doctrine only to those 'commercials' which are devoted in an obvious and meaningful way to the discussion of public issues."[20]

In June 1970, several antiwar groups in the San Francisco area filed a joint petition with the FCC, urging that military recruitment spots be declared a controversial issue of public importance. The groups argued in part that the fairness doctrine ought to apply to PSAs because "as opposed to normal commercial announcements, the broadcaster is making an editorial judgment in choosing the particular spot announcement and must therefore be more cognizant of his fairness obligation, to preserve his facilities as an 'uninhibited marketplace of ideas.' "[21] The FCC denied the complaint, reasoning that the issue with which the spots dealt was not the Vietnam war, but rather the power of the government to raise an army. This, it said, could not be considered a controversial issue.[22] The ruling was subsequently upheld by the U.S. Court of Appeals.

The latest decision bearing on the subject of public service advertising involved Business Executives Move for Viet Nam Peace, who complained to the FCC that broadcasters had violated the First Amendment by refusing to sell time to broadcast spot announcements expressing the group's views on the Vietnam conflict. They also complained that the stations' coverage of antiwar views failed to meet the requirements of the fairness doctrine. The FCC rejected the fairness doctrine challenge and also ruled that a broadcaster was not prohibited from having a policy of refusing to accept paid editorial advertisements by organizations like the complainants.

In Columbia Broadcasting System et al. v. the Democratic National Committee, the U.S. Supreme Court agreed with the Federal Communications Commission. The Court held that neither the Communications Act nor the First Amendment requires broadcasters to accept paid editorial advertisements.[23] If broadcasters are not required to accept paid advertising, it would hardly seem likely that they be required to accept public service advertising. Indeed, the vigor of the broadcasting industry's opposition is suggested by an advertisement in which Washington, D.C., newspaper readers—obviously including government officials—were told: "If everyone who disagrees with a television commercial were given free time to put on his own 'counter commercial,' then television's towers would turn into modern-day Towers of Babel, transmitting countless claims and counter-claims to bewildered viewers at home. The result: chaos. The television system we have today would disintegrate."[24]

Of course, a case-by-case assertion of fairness doctrine violations in specific instances is still an available recourse, but given the present composition of the Federal Communications Commission, that body at best is likely to be receptive only sporadically to the complaints of dissident groups. Moreover, even if the FCC were receptive, nothing requires broadcasters to balance coverage of controversial issues with PSAs expressing an opposing view; they may present the opposing view in any form they wish.

CONCLUSIONS

Although we shall return to this topic in Chapter 12, we tentatively conclude here that litigation and appeals to the Federal Communications Commission seem to be unproductive routes for excluded groups seeking to air PSAs. There are, of course, alternatives available to public service advertising on television. Some of the representatives of excluded groups interviewed concurred with the Choate organization that television advertising requires too much money and effort to be worthwhile. Some of these groups have been successful in placing advertisements in magazines and on the radio at the same time that their efforts to place television PSAs were being frustrated. The problem is that magazines and stations that are willing to accept the PSAs of dissident groups reach an audience which is most probably already in agreement with the groups' positions, which is why they are willing to run the spots. Thus, these groups find it difficult to spread their ideas beyond this closed circle to the larger world. Television exposure is one way such groups and ideas might receive a measure of legitimacy among the public at large rather than among those who are already predisposed to listen. The values and ideas these excluded groups are espousing are not necessarily superior to the values and ideas of those allowed free access, but this should not be a necessary condition for their dissemination.

One may ask whether public service advertising can be an appropriate means through which to communicate opinions and values. Is a 30- or 60-second spot a proper forum for the discussion of complex societal problems? True, it is sometimes difficult to present rational discussion of complex issues in 60 seconds. Instead, the producers of these spots tend to rely on auditory and visual stimuli to gain and keep the viewers' attention while attempting to persuade through an emotional appeal. This is the opinion of many groups that either do not engage in public service advertising or have made one effort and decided not to make any more PSAs. This position is also held by many of the networks and stations who refuse to air the spots produced by dissident groups, on the grounds that they are providing full coverage of the issue in question on their regular programming. However, some of those groups which have attempted to gain access through litigation argue that the only way to counter a spot announcement is with another spot announcement. Indeed, this is the rationale behind the recent counteradvertising movement. In their petition filed with the Federal Communications Commission, the San Francisco Women for Peace et al. argued, according to the FCC, that spot announcements, rather than news and discussion coverage, should be used to fulfill fairness doctrine obligations incurred by coverage of the Vietnam war because of the "more effective motivating factors inherent in an 'uninterrupted,' 'prepackaged message' which 'allows the sponsor . . . to prepare the announcements in such a manner as to have a desired psychological effect' rather than the 'straightforward manner aimed at persuading the listeners's rational sense' which is the way views are presented on news and talk programs."[25] We concur.

NOTES

1. "Gays Tell NBC Brass that Video Gays Tend to Treat Them Queerly," *Variety*, March 28, 1973.
2. "Gay Center Wins Pubserv. Spots at KNBC; Also Bid for a Regular Showcase," *Variety*, April 11, 1973.

3. Learning from its negative experiences with the Advertising Council and local stations, Public Communications, Inc., has revised its tactics and achieved a modicum of success. Its efforts are discussed in Chapter 12.

4. Letter from Robert B. Choate, director, Council on Children, Media and Merchandising, to station managers and network presidents, November 1972.

5. Ibid.

6. Letter from Robert D. Kasmire, vice-president, Public Relations, National Broadcasting Corporation, to Robert B. Choate, April 25, 1973.

7. Letter from Eleanor S. Applewhite, assistant general attorney, Columbia Broadcasting System to Robert B. Choate, June 8, 1973.

8. Ibid.

9. Letter from Grace M. Johnsen, vice-president, department of Broadcast Standards and Practices, American Broadcasting Company, to Robert B. Choate, May 1, 1973.

10. See 48 FCC 2d 1, *Fairness Report,* 1974, p. 1, n. 1. The document contains a historical survey of the doctrine and the FCC's latest interpretation of its meaning and intent.

11. 9 FCC 2d (1968), p. 940.

12. Ibid., p.943.

13. Attesting to the possible effects of PSAs, the president of the American Cancer Society claimed that returning antismoking commercials to the air in their pre-1971 abundance would save millions of lives (Washington *Post*, March 31, 1973).

14. 24 FCC 2d (1971), p. 743.

15. Ibid., pp. 748-49.

16. *Friends of the Earth v. FCC,* 449 F. 2d 1164 (D.C. Cir. 1971).

17. *Fairness Report,* 48 FCC 2d 1, 1974, p. 36.

18. Ibid., pp. 36-37.

19. Ibid., p. 37, n. 22.

20. Ibid., p. 39.

21. 24 FCC 2d (1971), p. 157. The characterization of the complaint is the FCC's.

22. Ibid., pp. 157-58.

23. 412 U.S. 94, 1973.

24. Full-page advertisement placed by the Television Information Office of the National Association of Broadcasters in the Washington *Post* and *Star News,* January 23, 1973.

25. 24 FCC 2d (1971), pp. 156-57.

CHAPTER 6

TECHNIQUES AND EFFECTS

The creation of public service advertising requires the expenditure of large amounts of money, time, and talent by the government, the Advertising Council, nonprofit organizations, and advertising agencies. A great many people are thus employed in producing and distributing PSAs which reach a great many more people by being broadcast over the networks and individual stations. It is not exaggerating to say that there is a public service advertising business whose purpose is to persuade and cajole the American people, and that the PSAs created by this business receive massive audience exposure. Thus, it becomes important to examine the persuasive techniques the producers of PSAs use and the possible effects of their products upon the public.

As with any commercial, the producers of PSAs have had to evolve techniques for most effectively using a 30- or 60-second time period as a method of persuasion. This chapter will discuss the techniques through the perceptions of the producers and then, using a variety of data, attempt to determine the possible effects of PSAs. The data on effects consist of the experiences of producers and station personnel with public reaction to particular PSAs and campaigns, a few studies on the impact of particular PSAs, and the results of a telephone poll conducted in Durham, North Carolina, and Washington, D.C., which attempted to elicit a general impression of public awareness of PSAs and the impact they might have.

PERSUASIVE TECHNIQUES

Given the constraints of the format within which they are working, what techniques do producers of PSAs use to increase the probable efficacy of their spots? The producers' intention is to create a spot which will have some unique aspect likely to gain viewers' immediate attention, to create awareness of a problem, to remain in the viewer's memory, and to motivate viewers to action. The following discussion concerns the producers' perceptions of the techniques that are likely to accomplish these goals. The discussion will necessarily be very general because, as the interviewees insisted, each problem requires a different approach or combination of approaches. These are merely several possible alternatives, and this discussion will be limited to techniques respondents themselves mentioned. In the next chapter, the actual techniques used in a representative sample of PSAs will be reported.

PSAs often attempt to persuade through an appeal to the viewer's emotions. One method used in past years, but now looked upon with disfavor, is the so-called scare tactic. Many of the subjects with which PSAs are concerned, such as drunk driving, drug abuse, and smoking, lend themselves to this technique. Producers using the scare tactic attempt to frighten viewers about the possible results of undesirable bahavior. Thus, there have been drunk driving PSAs with pictures of terrible accidents, and drug abuse spots graphically depicting an addict in the throes of withdrawal. According to PSA producers, the problem with this approach shown by communications research is that viewers are likely to ignore messages that could profoundly disturb them. For instance, in the case of antismoking spots, we were told "the more you frighten the smoker, the more anxious the smoker becomes and the more he will smoke to overcome his anxiety."

Another often used technique, humor or irony, is now considered a superior method of dealing with anxiety-arousing subjects such as smoking or drunk driving. It is believed that while viewers will ignore a disturbing message, they will pay attention to and remember a humorous or ironic one. The American Lung Association now presents such an antismoking message depicting the discomfort smokers inflict on nonsmokers.

Many of the interviewees stated that in presenting certain subjects it is most efficacious to create an atmosphere, character, or situation with which the average viewer is likely to identify. This is done by appealing to emotions and concepts the viewer values. Two of the best examples are a drunk driving spot produced by Grey Advertising for the Department of Transportation and a Red Cross spot produced by J. Walter Thompson. The Department of Transportation spot is entitled "Janie." It was the producer's intention to manipulate the viewers' emotions by having them identify with the characters, situations, and values invoked to such an extent that they would be shocked by the outcome, Janie's death at the hands of a drunk driver. The spot was supposed to heighten viewer awareness of drunk driving as a serious problem. The Red Cross's "Alice" used much the same approach, depicting a young female Red Cross volunteer visiting two elderly ladies. This was an attempt to transform the "fusty" image of the Red Cross through the symbol of a young girl. The spot provides little information about the Red Cross, but rather attempts, we were told, to "create a feeling of the Red Cross being whatever is needed within its community."

Many PSAs attempt to persuade viewers through appeals to their self-interest. Those in charge of the Savings Bond campaign found, through a study conducted by the Survey Research Center at the University of Michigan, that people's prime motivation for purchasing bonds was self-interest, with patriotism an entirely secondary factor. The Savings Bonds PSAs now emphasize the security and convenience of saving through the purchase of bonds. Similarly, the Red Cross developed the "Good Neighbor" theme to convey the idea that when no one else was willing or able to help, the Red Cross would be present. The theme thus implies that it is to the viewer's advantage to support the Red Cross in case he is ever in such a situation. The National Kidney Foundation also employed this tactic, emphasizing that "It Might Happen to You."

Guilt is another emotion that producers of PSAs invoke to achieve the desired response on the part of the viewer. Thus, the PSAs for the United Negro College Fund seek to evoke latent guilt feelings in the middle- and upper-class whites at whom they are aimed.

Many PSAs invoke authority figures in an effort to lend credibility to their messages. In general, these authority figures fall into two classes: those with expertise in the subject being discussed, and celebrities from other fields. There are various views regarding the efficacy of both types. According to an audiovisual director of a nonprofit organization, the presence of a doctor in an antismoking spot enhances its believability. A White House aide connected with PSAs observed that a PSA which features a government official just lecturing from behind a desk will most likely be ineffectual. Government experience with drug abuse spots has tended to show that peer pressure is a more effective technique than the use of adult authority figures.

As for celebrities, some of our respondents believe that they are useful because they gain viewers' attention, while others assert that they only continue to be used because they are traditional and because meeting famous people boosts the egos of the producers of the advertisements. An appearance in an uncontroversial PSA cannot harm the public image of a celebrity and most probably redounds to his or her credit—the celebrity becomes associated in the public mind with a "worthy cause." As an example, consider the case of the National Football League. Having abandoned its series of commercials for the National Clearing House for Drug Abuse Information because "its scope was too narrow," the NFL decided to offer its services to the National Center for Voluntary Action. During the 1972 football season, 22 of the league's players appeared in PSAs touting the various projects of the NCVA. The players volunteered their time, and the spots were produced at a low cost by the NFL's film branch and aired during time provided free to the league by the networks broadcasting the games. For a relatively small outlay of funds (estimated at less than $250,000) the NFL was able, through its players, to associate itself with positive action on such matters as the environment and drug abuse. Incidentally, the use of celebrities seems in this instance to have been effective: the NCVA claimed to have received over 250 letters a week from prospective volunteers as a result of the NFL's PSAs.[1]

Slogans are another way in which producers of PSAs seek to make their spots more memorable. The American Lung Association, for instance, took an idiomatic phrase, "It's a matter of life and death," and altered it slightly to "It's a Matter of Life and Breath." Many producers try to develop such short and catchy slogans. We offer a cacophony of them at the end of this chapter.

Finally, some PSAs attempt to increase impact by providing viewers with an address or telephone number through which they can obtain further information or donate money. Opinion is also divided on the efficacy of this tactic. The producers of the United Negro College Fund's PSAs assert that, since it takes three seconds for an address to register, it is better to use the time at the end of a PSA with a slogan, conveying an idea viewers are more likely to remember. They believe that viewers motivated to donate money will locate the correct address. The National Kidney Foundation, similarly, does not solicit funds directly through PSAs, believing that the function of a PSA is to make a viewer more receptive when approached in another manner.

EFFECTIVENESS

We have delineated a few of the techniques producers of PSAs employ to beguile and persuade viewers. For the most part, the producers operate on the basis of intuition, not really knowing which techniques are likely to be most effective. One way to determine the efficacy of commercial advertisements is by ascertaining whether sales of the promoted product increase. Such direct measurement of the effects of PSAs is hard to achieve, particularly if the producers have no clear idea where and when their spots are appearing on television. And even when PSAs may be presumed to be having the effects intended, there are often explanations which have nothing or very little to do with the PSA (for example, the increase in military enlistments during the recession that started in 1973). Consequently, the producers of PSAs enjoy more creative latitude than their counterparts making commercial advertisements. More importantly, many of the sponsors and makers of PSAs are uncertain about their products' actual impact.

The Advertising Council apparently has no doubt of the effectiveness of many of the campaigns it supports, or no compunction about claiming accomplishments. Its promotional material recounts such striking successes as receiving 7 million requests for booklets on the facts and problems of mental health and mental retardation from the National Association for Mental Health; publicizing and attracting recruits for the Peace Corps (now part of ACTION) in a very short time; increasing the number of donors to the United Negro College Fund by one-third; saving more than 750,000 lives since the inception of its Traffic Safety campaign in 1945 (as estimated by the National Safety Council); saving more than $17 billion in natural resources by reducing the incidence of forest fires from 5,000 per million visitors to forests to 176 per million; helping to prevent the 1958 recession from declining into a depression; and promoting the sale of Series E Saving Bonds to a 1972 all-time high of $5.9 billion—a rate of purchase that assertedly is still increasing.[2]

Problems arise when we seek more convincing evidence than that provided by the Advertising Council. The measurement of the effects PSAs may produce requires the expenditure of time and money with no guarantee that the results of surveys or other research tactics will be meaningful. Whereas advertising agencies routinely perform marketing analysis of commercial accounts, this is rarely done for PSAs. Most sponsors of PSAs have neither the time, money, nor expertise to attempt an analysis of effects. They do, however, sometimes have some rough measures of the impact of particular PSAs and campaigns through mail and telephone responses from the public. One of the big campaigns of the Office of Education was for technical education training. Conducted under Advertising Council auspices, it consisted of one commercial showing comedian Tommy Smothers talking to a computer. At its conclusion viewers were urged to write for the booklet *Careers.* The Office of Education reportedly received 102,000 letters in one month and over 2 million since the campaign's inception. Enrollment in secondary education programs has supposedly risen in direct proportion to exposure to the spot. One of its originators believes the campaign was successful because people want and need jobs, so the program's objectives and the public's changing career aspirations coincided.

Officials connected with the Department of Transportation's campaign against drunk driving report that the number of requests for information has quintupled since the campaign began and an address to contact was provided; requests now exceed 1,000 in a slow month. Similarly, an executive of the Council of Better Business Bureaus told us that local bureaus were swamped with more complaints than they could handle after PSAs appeared urging viewers to call with their complaints. This apparent deluge took place even though the bureau tries to ensure in its advertisements that the focus is on sleazy fly-by-night operators. Indeed, the bureau revised its initial approach, which apparently "made all businessmen look like crooks."

ACTION, which established WATS lines for prospective recruits in various parts of the country, recorded a dramatic increase in calls where PSAs were aired. The antidrug campaign, in which the National Football League and the baseball leagues aired their own advertisements during their games, reportedly generated about 30,000 inquiries weekly at the Clearing House for Drug Abuse—the peak being achieved during the football season. One reason the NFL was approached was to circumvent the networks which, the campaign's leaders believed, were not devoting enough prime time to the PSAs. However, inspiring inquiries is not synonymous with diminishing the incidence of drug abuse. In NFL PSAs the players' statements were identical; and credibility may have been further strained by the inability of viewers, especially drug-taking youths, to equate themselves with highly paid professional athletes—especially given periodic stories about the latter's use and abuse of stimulants. Perhaps relatedly, the Heroin Hotline, which, in a separate set of PSAs, viewers were requested to call if they wished to report their local "pusher," initially received many crank calls—certainly an indication that the PSAs have some sort of effect, although not always the one intended.

Some sponsors attempt to elicit opinions from local affiliates as to the impact of particular campaigns in their region. On the whole, however, while many producers of PSAs engage in speculation concerning possible effects and base their techniques upon this speculation, they often remain uninformed about actual effects; they prefer to expend their limited funds on the campaigns themselves, rather than on research to determine their implications and effects.

Thus, the producers often base their techniques upon conventional wisdom as to what might be effective and upon what appeals to them personally. Yet pretesting public campaigns occassionally proves the producers' assumptions and expectations wrong. For instance, it would seem reasonable to direct PSAs for the United Negro College Fund at blacks who would be most likely to contribute. Yet, research showed that middle- and upper-class whites constitute the majority of contributors. Moreover, one would assume that, among whites, the liberals would be the largest contributors to the fund. The survey indicated that those voting for Nixon in 1972 were five times as likely to contribute as those voting for McGovern. Based upon this information, the producers changed their techniques in order to appeal to those most likely to contribute. Another instance of the difference between producers' perceptions and public reaction is the energy conservation campaign. The producers felt that since the energy shortage was being discussed as a crisis situation, they could rally the American public to save energy by appealing to patriotic instincts. Pretesting found this not to be the case, and the campign instead used the "Don't be Fuelish" theme, which emphasizes the material advantage to the viewer of conserving energy.

Some of the most sophisticated research has been performed for the armed services. Not patriotism, not access to guns, but the desire to learn a skill and travel were found to be the most important reasons for volunteering. Surveys also discovered that pay, other benefits, and an urge to build themselves up physically motivate people to join the army. PSAs consequently emphasize the acquisition of skills and travel opportunities and show rugged outdoor types who appear to be well paid and relishing such benefits of military life as the companionship of delectable females.

The academic study of the effects of mass communication has yielded a variety of conflicting theories and, for the most part, has been inconclusive.[3] Those who have attempted to assess the impact of PSAs through the use of social science techniques have faced the same problems as those researching the impact of any other mass communications medium. The situation is complicated by the fact that PSAs are one of the few examples of the conscious use of television to persuade; therefore, researchers ideally should be able to discover direct causal relations between the messages and changes in opinions, attitudes, or behavior patterns. However, so many other variables that are extremely difficult to control impinge on the research that this becomes virtually impossible. Even so, the research on the effects of PSAs has been limited for the most part to attempting to establish the impact of specific PSAs and particular campaigns.

The incapacity of some PSAs to achieve immediate results in the desired direction can result from several factors. These include inadequacies in the campaign, misconceived appeals in particular spots, and the arousing of those gorgons, selective exposure, selective perception, and selective retention. Thus, the government's various antidrug campaigns, whose purposes seem to be to limit drug intake by provoking anxiety and fear among viewers, have periodically encountered criticism on the basis of inappropriate messages and concomitant ineffectiveness. One study elicited disbelief from students who viewed them as "unenlightened preaching from the 'Establishment.' "[4] Another study reported "a significant contradiction between young people's experiences with drugs which have been helpful and meaningful, and the government's point of view that all or most drug use is bad and dangerous."[5]

Research on reaction to drug abuse PSAs has also been conducted at the University of Connecticut. Groups of students were shown one of five PSAs from the National Clearing House for Drug Abuse Information and were asked to indicate their reactions.[6] The study concluded that "three major independent dimensions underlie student perceptions of televised anti-drug abuse advertisements: how personally relevant the message content seems to be; how novel and exciting the manner of presentation is; and, how disturbing and emotional the message strategy seems."[7] Since memory of the message cannot be equated with changes in attitude or behavior as a result of the message, the study roughly measures what techniques may have impact on the viewer, but not which have the most impact. Moreover, the study is subject to the limitations of all research conducted in a laboratorylike atmosphere: the situation introduces several variables which would not be present if a person were viewing television and happened to be exposed to a PSA. Perhaps to rectify such defects and improve the effectiveness of antidrug PSAs, the Marketing Science Institute, associated with the Harvard Business School, and using funds provided by the National Institute of Mental Health, recently completed a special project entitled "Experimentation to Improve Pretesting of Anti-Drug Abuse Education and Information Campaigns."[8]

A study of antismoking PSAs tended to support "the principle that mass communications, including those presented on television, are greatly limited in their ability to affect behavior."[9] The data from questionnaires showed that those who felt that PSAs had affected them were already inclined to cease smoking, and of those who were considering stopping, half indicated they had been affected by the PSAs. Furthermore, although the great majority of smokers agreed that their habit posed a health hazard, they were not attempting to break the habit.[10] This indicates that PSAs can penetrate the viewers' consciousness with their messages, in this case by contributing to the idea that smoking is hazardous; they can also reinforce behavior predilections; but they are unlikely to change behavior.

A study attempting to assess the impact of family-planning messages disseminated through television, radio, and print was conducted from November 1970 through May 1971 in four cities in the United States.[11] Although the advertisements dealt with controversial subjects, there was no great negative reaction from the four communities. Most respondents surveyed remembered being exposed to the spots, and significant recruitment of new patients to birth control clinics occurred. This lends credence to the assertion that television is the best way to reach a mass audience, that consciousness of a problem can be raised and interest canalized through television PSAs. However, the advertisements did not seem to change behavior. The rate of decline of unwanted births in the four cities was actually slowed because, the investigators speculate, the advertisements made women more willing to admit the birth was unwanted; but the birth rate dropped no faster than in cities not part of the experiment.[12]

From June 1971 to March 1972, the Insurance Institute for Highway Safety conducted a saturation campaign over cable television in a test city using six PSAs designed to encourage viewers to wear safety seat belts.[13] It was estimated that the average viewer of the cable system saw one or another of the messages two or three times a week.[14] The institute claims that "the campaign was equivalent to the type of major advertising effort which companies use to promote a new product."[15] Observations, by observers stationed at strategic points in the cities, of actual use of seat belts were recorded before, during, and after the campaign. There was, however, no observed increase in the use of seat belts. Indeed, the data indicate that "the campaign had no effect whatsoever on safety belt use."[16]

In view of the fact that the sponsors of the campaign had far more control over placement of the PSAs and the viewers were exposed far more frequently than is usually the case with a public service campaign, the evidence strongly suggests that public service advertising is generally not an effective way to change deeply ingrained behavior. However, this conclusion may be mitigated by the techniques and quality of the commercials used. The PSAs were not of the best technical quality. Moreover, the thrust of the campaign was "to emphasize the efficacy of saftey belts in decreasing the probability of disfigurement and disability."[17] Accordingly, the PSAs featured people injured or disfigured by automobile accidents in which they were not wearing seat belts. It seems to us that such an approach is more likely to cause the viewer to avoid or ignore the message than accede to it.

In 1972, the United States Army conducted a telephone poll of 150 respondents (males aged 17 to 21) in each of five major metropolitan areas to determine the impact of army television, radio, and print advertising.[18] Among other results, the survey found that 60 percent of the respondents remembered having seem an army PSA. Recall of "advertising copy" and slogan was higher than recall of subject content or message. Television PSAs were the most often recalled. Between 4 and 5 percent of all respondents made an effort to obtain further information, and most respondents indicated that they would join the air force or the navy, rather than the army.[19] The evidence indicates that the advertising could be recalled, but resulted in neither attitude nor behavior changes.

Finally, to conclude our litany of research conducted by others, one study seemingly runs counter to this general picture of the relative inefficacy of PSAs in producing significant behavior changes. A one-month information campaign consisting of four televised PSAs, radio and newspaper advertisements, and a direct-mail campaign was conducted in Quincy, Illinois, during May 1972 to increase the levels of knowledge and influence attitudes towards pesticide labels and the safe use of pesticides. A panel of respondents was interviewed before and another panel after the campaign to determine information, attitude, and behavioral intent with regard to pesticides. Comparable interviews, used as a control mechanism, were conducted in Decatur, Illinois, where there was no pesticide information campaign. About one-fourth of those interviewed in the test community after the end of the campaign remembered having seen or heard the campaign slogan. These respondents also possessed more information about pesticides and expressed the intention of being more careful with them than did the respondents in the control city.[20] The only definite accomplishment of the campaign was to increase the level of information concerning pesticides; there is no proof, aside from the professed intentions of the respondents, that behavior actually changed as a result of exposure to the campaign.

Dissatisfied with this research, we embarked on a modest study of our own. Rather than attempting to assess the effects of a particular campaign, we tried to obtain an idea of the general immediate impression held by viewers of public service advertising on television. We conducted a telephone poll in Washington, D.C., and Durham, North Carolina, during April 1973, obtaining 100 usable responses in each city. Respondents were asked 11 questions, 8 related to PSAs and 3 attempting to establish demographic data (sex, race, age).

We first asked respondents whether they knew what a public service commercial was. We felt, erroneously as it transpired, that people would more readily respond if the term "commercial" was used instead of "advertisement," and "commercial" was used throughout the poll. Some 35.5 percent of all respondents knew what a PSA was. Of course, the fact that a viewer is unaware of the distinction between a commercial advertisement and a PSA does not mean that PSAs have no impact on him. People who do not know what a PSA is are just as likely to be affected by one as people who do know. The question was intended to establish a mutual understanding of the subject between poller and respondent. Those who claimed not to know what a PSA was were given a definition by the poller.

In question 2, the respondents were asked whether they remembered having seen any PSAs; 47.5 percent replied that they had, while a majority could not immediately remember having seen one.

Question 3 asked the respondents who remembered having seen one or more PSAs which particular ones they recalled. Responses fell into ten categories. In number of mentions, they rank as follows: health, environment, local/miscellaneous, drugs, community welfare services, business/consumer, brotherhood/appreciation, humanitarian, education, and military. It is interesting to compare the results of this question with the results of question 10 of the questionnaire we sent to television stations, which asked broadcasters to list any PSAs which had received a response from the public. The answers to this question fell into the same categories. In rank order, they were: education, community welfare services, health, business/consumer, drugs, environment, local, humanitarian, brotherhood/appreciation, military, and disadvantaged. Health and community welfare services were ranked high by both broadcasters and viewers. Question 11 on the station questionnaire asked broadcasters how they accounted for the greater response to these PSAs. When the answers were categorized, about half the broadcasters indicated that these PSAs have more impact because they appeal to the self-interest of the viewer. From the results of both the questionnaire and the poll, it would appear that PSAs appealing to viewers' self-interest would be recalled most frequently and elicit the greatest response.

When asked what elements of PSAs they recalled, 27.8 percent of viewers mentioned such things as setting or plot, music, action, or slogan, and 21.6 percent remembered specific information. From the plethora of messages and techniques, it therefore appears that something gets through to a majority of viewers who became conscious of the messages of at least some PSAs.

About half of the respondents could recall characters from PSAs. Such characters included actors, famous national and local personalities, and animated figures. Most people remembered an actor creating a character. Since producers often attempt to create identification with characters, the techniques seem to be effective, at least insofar as recall is concerned.

Question 6 attempted to measure behavior produced by PSAs and to ascertain whether the use of addresses and telephone numbers is effective. No respondents recalled having called a toll-free number, but 5 percent of all respondents said they had written to an address for further information. It seems the advertising executive who asserted that the time needed for an address to register could be better occupied by a slogan was correct, especially since slogan recall was relatively high.

Question 7 asked respondents whether they had ever been prompted by a PSA to donate money to a cause or organization. Approximately 15 percent of the respondents replied in the affirmative. This suggests that some PSAs can influence people to take action. Indeed, when we asked respondents whether they felt thay had recently been affected by PSAs in any manner, 24 percent responded affirmatively. Of this 24 percent, 34.2 percent were prompted to take action such as donating funds, 34.2 percent felt their awareness of a problem had increased, 18.4 percent were reminded of a problem, and 13.2 percent gained specific information.

We suspect that respondent awareness and reactions to public service advertising are seriously underestimated in our study—a telephone survey that roused viewers from a quiet evening of television watching and posed awkward, even embarrassing, questions about a topic not of immediate concern to them.

PSAs may not be easy to recall immediately upon demand—few advertisements are—yet they are insidiously pervasive, and many of their slogans are ingrained in the public consciousness. Consider how many of the following are at least vaguely familiar:

Give To The College Of Your Choice.
Don't Crawl Under A Rock. Get Into ACTION.
Don't Forget. Hire The Vet.
Kick The Habit.
I Mind Very Much If You Smoke.
It's A Matter Of Life And Breath.
When A Problem Drinker Drives, It's Your Problem.
Fight Cancer With A Check-up And A Check.
Thanks To You It's Working. The United Way.
When You're Busted For Drugs Over There, You're In For The Hassle Of Your Life.
Don't Be Fuelish.
Take Stock In America. Buy U.S. Savings Bonds.
People Start Pollution. People Can Stop It.
Children By Choice. Not Chance.
Have A College Grad's Career Without Four Years Of College.
Sign of the Good Neighbor. The Red Cross.
A Mind Is A Terrible Thing To Waste.
What We Need Money Can't Buy. We Need You.
Only You Can Prevent Forest Fires.
VD Is For Everybody.
Every Litter Bit Hurts.
America. It Only Works As Well As We Do.

Our telephone poll, plus the other studies of PSA effects, point to a relatively high degree of consciousness penetration by public service campaigns. It is difficult, if not impossible, to measure tangible effects or establish a causal relationship between message and effect. It does appear, however, that many of the messages contained in PSAs get through to viewers. No wonder! PSAs are ubiquitous. Yet they do not appear capable of changing many people's behavior. What they apparently can do is canalize predispositions and reinforce existing behavior. We must therefore analyze the content of a representative sample of PSAs to discover what predispositions they are canalizing and what behavior they are reinforcing.

NOTES

1. "NFL Taps People Who Care," Washington *Post,* December 10, 1972.

2. As recounted in the Advertising Council, *Free Enterprise's Effective Communications Machine* (New York,n.d..).

3. See, for example, Gerhart D. Wiebe, "Two Psychological Factors in Media Audience Behavior," *Public Opinion Quarterly* 33 (Winter 1969-70): 523-36; Herbert H. Hyman and Paul B. Sheatsley, "Some Reasons Why Information Campaigns Fail," *Public Opinion Quarterly* 11 (Fall 1947): 412-22, both of which are of particular relevance; and the standard work on the subject (which, however, excludes television commercials from its ambit), Joseph T. Klapper, *The Effects of Mass Communication* (New York: The Free Press, 1960).

4. Donald L. Kanter, "Some Aspects of the Broadcast Anti-Drug Program," abstract of paper presented at the Twenty-Sixth Conference of the American Association for Public Opinion Research, *Public Opinion Quarterly* 35 (Fall 1971): 459.

5."Anti-Drug Campaign Said Faulty," Washington *Post*, November 2, 1972.

6. William J. McEwen and Gerhard J. Hanneman, "Public Service Advertising and Social Problems: The Case of Drug Abuse Prevention" (Storrs: University of Connecticut, mimeo, pp. 1-12).

7. Ibid., p. 7.

8. Michael L. Ray, Scott Ward, and Jerome B. Read, *New Directions for Advertising Pretesting Research* (Cambridge, Mass.: Marketing Science Institute, N.D.).

9. M. Timothy O'Keefe, "The Anti-Smoking Commercials: A Study of Television's Impact on Behavior," *Public Opinion Quarterly* 35 (Summer 1971): 248.

10. Ibid.

11. J. Richard Udry, "A Mass Media Experiment in Family Planning," paper presented at American Association for Public Opinion Research Conference, Asheville, N.C. May 1973.

12. Ibid., p. 6.

13. Leon S. Robertson et al., "A Controlled Study of the Effect of Television Messages on Safety Belt Use" (Washington, D.C.: Insurance Institute for Highway Safety, June 1972).

14. Ibid., p. 9.

15. Ibid.

16. Ibid.

17. Ibid., p. 4.

18. "A Survey of Awareness, Penetration and Believability of U.S. Army Advertising," (Philadelphia: Consumer/Industrial Research Service, December 1972), pages unnumbered.

19. Ibid., "Executive Summary" section.

20. See Rodolfo N. Salcedo et al., "A Successful Information Campaign on Pesticides," *Journalism Quarterly* 51 (Spring 1974): 91-95 ff.

CHAPTER

7

THE EXPLICIT CONTENT OF PSAs

In order to speculate intelligently on the effects of public service advertisements upon the attitudes or behavior of people exposed to them, we need data drawn from the content of a representative sample of PSAs. Such data can also tell us the kinds of PSAs which appear on television and their assorted technical aspects. To obtain such a representative sample of PSAs it was necessary to monitor television stations. We therefore recorded all the PSAs broadcast during a one-week period, April 15 through April 21, 1973, over two stations, WRDU-TV, a UHF, NBC affiliate located in Durham, North Carolina, and WDCA-TV, a UHF, independent station located in Washington, D.C. Forty-four individual PSAs were recorded in Washington and 50 in Durham. The actual number of PSAs shown is much higher, but we eliminated local announcements read by an announcer while a slide was displayed; and no matter how often a PSA was shown during the week we only counted it once. In addition, no network PSAs broadcast over NBC-affiliate WRDU were recorded. Consequently, the difference between the two stations was reduced to the size of the market in which they are located.

Recording PSAs is an onerous task that we were compelled to approach in two ways. At WDCA in Washinton, D.C., we went to the station every day and obtained the following day's logs showing when PSAs would be shown. We then monitored the station continually while it was on the air, videotaping every PSA. The logs proved to be a rough guide only, for often a PSA would appear several minutes before or after it was scheduled, and sometimes it would not appear at all. At WRDU in Durham, a station to which we acquired access because of personal acquaintance with the owner, we arranged for the program director to provide us with copies of every non-network PSA shown during the week. We checked the logs to ensure our collection was complete.

The analysis of the PSAs was done on two levels: explicit and implicit content. The explicit level identifies such aspects of a PSA as length, sponsor, and topic; the implicit level is concerned with the underlying messages that may be communicated. This chapter deals with the explicit level.

PSA TYPE

PSAs are either 10, 20, 30, or 60 seconds long. The shorter spots usually consist of a slide with which one or two sentences or a slogan is read by an announcer. Obviously, such PSAs are limited in what they can achieve, serving chiefly as a reminder to viewers. Producers consider 30- and 60-second PSAs to be a better format for achieving their goals because they permit the use of persuasive techniques. The majority of PSAs in our sample, 64 percent, were 60 seconds in length; 34 percent were 30 seconds. No 20-second PSAs, and only one 10-second one, were recorded. The producers' preference for the longer format seems to be reflected in the PSAs available to stations and those which are broadcast. Moreover, since commercial advertisements are usually 30 or 60 seconds and PSAs fill unsold commercial time, it is logical that they should be for the most part the same length as the commercials.

The topic of the PSA is important: it indicates those subjects with which PSAs deal, as well as those which they ignore. Our list of eight topics was compiled from an analysis of Advertising Council campaigns and our own observations of sample PSAs. Following is a list of the topics, examples of each, and the percentage of our sample PSAs that fell into each category.

Health and safety: These PSAs urge viewers to take action to protect their well-being. Health PSAs are also often solicitations for funds for health research. Viewers are urged to use seat belts, get a checkup for cancer, or contribute to the National Kidney Foundation. PSAs for health and safety compose 43.5 percent of our sample.

Environment: These PSAs point out the adverse effects of man upon the environment and, depending on the sponsor, sometimes urge viewers to take corrective action. An example of this type is a Keep America Beautiful PSA. This category made up 11.7 percent of our sample.

Community welfare: The purpose of these PSAs is to inform viewers of the services performed by either government agencies or nonprofit organizations within the local community. A YMCA PSA would be included in this category. About 9.6 percent of our sample fell into this category.

Business-consumer: These PSAs explain the role of business in the society, the relation of the consumer to business, and how the consumer may benefit from this relationship. An example would be a PSA on product safety or one informing the viewer of the activities of the Better Business Bureau. They compose 7.4 percent of our sample.

Military: 7.4 percent of our sample are military recruitment spots.

Humanitarianism: We classified PSAs which solicit funds for disadvantaged peoples in underdeveloped countries as humanitarian. An example would be a Save the Children PSA. This was 6.7 percent of our sample.

Disadvantaged: These PSAs (6.4 percent) solicit support for the organizations which aid the disadvantaged in the United States. An example would be an ACTION PSA.

Education: Such PSAs urge viewer support of higher education, as in a United Negro College Fund spot. Just 2.1 percent of our sample were in this category.

Miscellaneous: Of our sample, 4.3 percent did not fall into any of these eight topics.

This breakdown indicates a domination of the public service advertising field by organizations concerned with the health and safety of the viewer. It would seem from our data that PSAs are more often concerned with subjects that directly affect, or could directly affect, the viewer, than with more distant concerns.

The identification of the sponsors of the PSAs actually broadcast provides the best way to determine which groups actually receive air time. The sponsors of our sample PSAs and, we would venture, of the great majority of all PSAs can be divided into five categories: governmental agencies such as the Department of Health, Education, and Welfare; national service organizations, such as the American Cancer Society; local service organizations, such as the Children's Hospital in Washington; international service organizations, such as CARE; and religious organizations, such as the Franciscans. National service organizations sponsored 56.4 percent of the PSAs in our sample; government agencies, 25.5 percent; local groups, 8.5 percent; international service organizations, 2.1 percent; and religious organizations, 1.1 percent. Although they are technically not PSAs, 5.3 percent of our sample were sponsored by corporations and logged and broadcast as PSAs, and 1.9 percent of our sample were sponsored by organizations which did not fall under any of the five categories, such as the North Carolina Bar Association. The fact that 84 percent of our sample was sponsored by government and well-established nonprofit organizations is indicative of their influence on public service advertising. Only 15 percent of our sample PSAs were sponsored by the Advertising Council. The percentages of PSAs from govermental agencies and the Advertising Council would have been increased had network PSAs been included.

Of our sample, 17 percent were produced by local groups, 83 percent by national groups. Local groups have greater access to television stations than these figures would indicate. Their programs and activities are often announced during a block of similar PSAs read by an announcer over a slide. This type of exposure, however, does not have the same persuasive quality as a filmed spot. Moreover, a long block of PSAs can be more readily turned off or ignored by viewers than a 30- or 60-second filmed PSA. The data indicate that, at least insofar as the monitored stations are concerned, local groups cannot and do not compete on an equal basis for time with national groups. This is probably not a function of any decision on the part of the station gatekeeper, but is probably due to local groups' lack of funds and media expertise. Local groups obtaining professionally produced PSAs from a national organization, and adding their address or logo, would more likely have success in obtaining publicity.

PSAs are intended either for the population as a whole or for a specific audience. Many producers assert that they can better convey their message through several PSAs aimed at different audiences. The Advertising Council directs all its PSAs at a general audience. Through an analysis of our sample PSAs, we attempted to determine which of these techniques is most often used. The majority of PSAs, 58.5 percent, were directed at a general audience, while 41.5 percent were directed at such specific audiences as adults or parents, children, and senior citizens.

Is the PSA "responseable"? That is, does it provide an address or telephone number to which viewers can respond directly? More than one-third (38.3 percent) gave an address to which the viewers could write for further information. (It might be mentioned that many PSAs which do provide an address do not give the viewer enough time to write it down, even if pen and paper are at hand.) PSAs often solicit viewers' support or money, or urge them to obtain further information about a problem, and then do not provide an address to which they can respond. This is perhaps an effective technique, given the PSAs' seeming ability to create awareness but not necessarily action on the part of viewers.

It seems to us that PSAs can create viewer awareness of a problem, change viewers' attitudes about a problem, or prompt viewers to take action to ameliorate a problem. The three are certainly not mutually exclusive, and it is often hard to categorize PSAs according to these goals. It does seem, however, that each PSA has a main thrust, and this is the basis upon which we made the categorizations. The majority of the PSAs, 62.8 percent of our sample, appeared intended to produce some form of activity; 21.3 percent provided information to create awareness; and the other 16 percent were intended to affect attitudes. A possible explanation for this distribution lies in the dominance of the public service field by well-established nonprofit organizations and the government. Our interviews with PSA producers led to the discovery that the producers often evolve a three-stage campaign to deal with a problem. First, they attempt to create awareness by providing information about both the sponsoring organization and the problem with which it is concerned. The second stage attempts to affect viewers' attitudes so that they will become responsive to the appeal of the organization. The third stage urges the viewers to act in a certain manner to contribute to the solution of the problem. Because governmental agencies and well-established nonprofit organizations often do not need to create awareness of their existence or the problems with which they are concerned, they are able to bypass the first two stages and concentrate upon the third, urging viewers to action.

STRUCTURE

Famous personalities are often employed in PSAs to attract viewers' attention and in the hope that the celebrities' popularity will be reflected on the sponsoring organizations. As discussed in the previous chapter, opinion is divided as to the efficacy of this technique. In our sample, 17 percent of PSAs featured celebrities.

Many of the producers to whom we talked stressed the importance of the proper narrator, both to lend authority to the message and to create a particular ambience. All but 4 percent of the PSAs had a narrator, and almost all the narrators sounded as if they were white (90.8 percent), male (89.7 percent), and neither particularly young nor particularly old (73.6 percent). PSAs are produced for the most part by white, middle-aged males and overwhelmingly employ white, middle-aged males as narrators.

We use the term "actors" to apply to people appearing in PSAs, of which there are four types: actors portraying characters in realistic situations (73.6 percent); actual people in realistic situations, usually in crowd scenes which are obviously not staged (24.1 percent); actors in studios in what are obviously not realistic situations (1.1 percent); and animated characters (1.1 percent). Since the producers intend to create identifications with the characters, it is only logical that PSAs should feature, in the main, either real people or actors portraying characters.

Most of the PSAs in our sample, 47.3 percent, featured only males, 45.9 percent showed both sexes, and 6.8 percent only females. Most often the actors were exclusivelywhite (59.5 percent) or of both races (25.7 percent); and 14.9 percent were all black. As with the narrators, the characters are most often white and male. In terms of age, young adults (28.4 percent) or children (23 percent) were most often featured. There are two reasons for the predilection of producers for children. First, childhood symbolizes hope, innocence, and the future; and children are supposedly more honest and direct and therefore more credible. Second, children, being obviously more vulnerable and in need of care than adults, are often featured in humanitarian and disadvantaged PSAs to evoke viewers' sympathy.

Music is often used to add to the mood of a PSA. The majority of our sample, 61.7 percent, contained music.

A slogan is viewed by producers as a way of gaining viewers' attention, as well as remaining in their memories. Almost 40 percent of the PSAs included a slogan—a figure which would be considerably higher were network PSAs included.

One method of persuasion is to present a threatening subject in a humorous or ironic manner, in order to catch the viewer off-guard. Only 19.1 percent of the PSAs in our sample, however, could be considered humorous or ironic. This may be explained by the fact that many producers consider it inappropriate to deal with a serious subject in a light manner.

As has been discussed in both this and previous chapters, producers, in order better to convey their messages, often attempt to create a character with whom the viewers will identify. It is not necessary that the character have the same age, race, and sex characteristics as the viewer. Rather, the identification stems from the character's being involved in a situation with which the viewer is likely to empathize. Thus, by human identification, we mean that the characters and situations are drawn from elements of the viewers' experiences. In fact, 56.4 percent of our sample featured a character with whom viewers were likely to identify.

CHAPTER

8

SOCIALIZATION, THE CIVIC CULTURE, AND PSAs

The evidence presented thus far suggests the following:

There is a "public service advertising business nexus" whose existence depends upon, and entails the expenditure of, a great deal of time, money, and talent.

Those who are not members of this nexus find it extremely difficult to produce PSAs and, once they are produced, to persuade broadcasters to air them.

The people involved in the business have devised a variety of techniques which they believe will increase the persuasiveness of their product.

The networks and the local stations, although not according PSAs preferential treatment, still broadcast so vast a number as to ensure that PSAs have massive audience exposure.

The limited research performed to this point suggests that PSAs do not often change behavior.

But PSAs can canalize viewers' predispositions and reinforce existing behavior.

This last point, we believe, justifies and even necessitates a study of public service advertising. There have been a few desultory investigations of particular stages of the funneling process, most notably of the Advertising Council, by public interest-oriented groups disgruntled by their failure to gain access. One or two attempts have been made to measure the direct effects of PSAs on individuals and to elucidate the treatment accorded PSAs by local stations. Our study encompasses and transcends all of these efforts by describing the funneling process in its entirety, from the inception of a campaign to its eventual airing and its possible effects upon viewers. Yet, we feel there are more important aspects to public service advertising. It is our contention that primarily through PSAs a particular set of political attitudes and orientations is being conveyed to the American public. The rest of this book explicates and elaborates on this fundamental assertion.[1]

One of the basic problems faced by any society is the legitimation of its authority system. Legitimacy involves the capacity of the system to engender and maintain the belief that existing institutions and authorities meet the interests of the members of the society, thus leading to the acceptance of the authority the leaders exercise. Moreover, in order for a society to continue to function with stability, there must also be basic social attitudes which govern interaction among the followers and the followers' interaction with the leaders. Socialization is one of the important ways by which a society's members can be led to develop and hold the appropriate attitudes governing social interaction and to accept the existing authority system.

Socialization may take place on an overt level through the conscious attempts of authorities in church, school, and home to inculcate in children the values necessary for them to be functioning members of the society. It can also take place on a covert level, through the transmission, by these and other agencies, of messages which have no overt political content, yet have political relevance. Political culture "is acquired in a subtle, non-deliberate way, often in a context which seems totally void of political stimuli yet is often rife with political consequences."[2]

The mass media are part of the socialization process on both the overt and covert levels. And it seems to us that PSAs, as part of the substance of the mass media, contribute significantly to the socialization process. Although for the most part they appear to lack obvious political content, they transmit messages from America's elite and their institutions to the members of the society. They are important for their explicit content and the specific actions they demand of individual viewers. They are even more important because of the values they contain, the images they collectively propound of authority and American institutions, their portrayals of the nature and causes of societal problems, and the solutions they designate for these problems. Indeed, we believe that public service advertising should be considered as one way in which the American public is imbued with the values and attitudes that contribute to the current functioning and stability of the American political system.

The Civic Culture by Gabriel A. Almond and Sidney Verba offers a felicitous way to approach and analyze the content and probable effects of public service advertising.[3] We shall therefore give a general outline of the book's theory and then use it as a fulcrum for analyzing the underlying content of PSAs.

Almond and Verba attempt to distinguish between those elements characterizing a democratic polity with a history of political stability and those characterizing democracies which seem to be in a perpetual state of crisis.

They do not devote much attention to the formal aspects of the society, such as constitutions, laws, and governmental apparatus, nor are they concerned to any great extent with the society's elites. Rather, they focus upon the general citizenry in an attempt to determine those factors whose presence may lead to political stability and whose absence, to instability.

Almond and Verba structure their analysis around the designation of three types of orientations among members of a society: the parochial, the subject, and the participant. The parochial is divorced from the government, neither contributing to the governmental process, nor being affected by governmental decisions. The subject is oriented toward output and is "aware of specialized governmental authority; he is affectively oriented to it, perhaps taking pride in it, perhaps disliking it." The participant is oriented toward "both the input and output aspects of the political system." Almond and Verba assert that the "citizen" of a democratic polity is a "particular mix of participant, subject, and parochial orientations." He "is not only oriented toward active participation in politics, but is subject to law and authority and is a member of more diffuse primary groups."[4]

Consequently, in the civic culture, all three orientations are present at the same time; "participant political orientations combine with and do not replace subject and parochial orientations."[5] The result is "a balanced political culture in which political activity, involvement, and rationality exist [among the citizenry] but are balanced by passivity, traditionality, and commitment to parochial values."[6]

This balance between involvement and noninvolvement composes the essence of the civic culture. It has three aspects: a balance between instrumental and affective orientations citizens hold toward the societal system; a balance between consensus and cleavage within that system; and a balance between citizen passivity and participation.

Obviously Almond and Verba look with approval upon the civic culture and upon the United States as embodying its closest approximation—at least they did in 1963 when the book was published. Equally obviously, the book, pioneering and innovative as it was, is not without significant flaws.[7] One of the most obvious is the term "balance" which, as they use it, is protean and impossible to operationalize. Their dubious equation of stable with effective democracy is another serious problem. Nonetheless, the civic culture provides a useful way of looking at public service advertising. Do PSAs promote consensus or cleavage? Do they encourage affective or instrumental orientations? What sort of political participation, if any, do PSAs stimulate? In answering these questions, we can delve more deeply into both the explicit and underlying contents of the commercials and speculate (we hope usefully) on their overall political effects. In so doing, we draw for illustration upon the PSAs from our sample, supplemented by others which have appeared on television with some frequency during the past few years.

NOTES

1. For an argument that the analyses of the political effects of the mass media have defined effects far too narrowly see Colin Seymour-Ure, *The Political Impact of Mass Media* (Beverly Hills, Calif.: Sage Publications, 1974).

2. Roberta Sigel, "Assumptions About the Learning of Political Values," *The Annals of the American Academy of Political and Social Science* 361 (1965): 4.

3. Gabriel A. Almond and Sidney Verba, *The Civic Culture* (Princeton: Princeton University Press, 1963).

4. Ibid., pp. 19, 20.

5. Ibid., p. 31.

6. Ibid., p. 23.

7. See Stein Rokkan's review of the book in *The American Political Science Review* 58 (1964): 676-79.

CHAPTER

9

PSAs AND CONSENSUS-CLEAVAGE

According to Almond and Verba, some cleavage within a society is a good thing for the operation of democratic politics. After all, "too much agreement would mitigate against the enforcement of elite responsiveness." They seem more concerned, however, with the dangerous potential of conflict and the importance of consensus. "If there is no consensus within society, there can be little potentiality for the peaceful resolution of political differences that is associated with the democratic process." How, then, is cleavage managed? It "is accomplished by subordinating conflicts on the political level to some higher, overarching attitudes of solidarity."[1]

To determine whether PSAs promote consensus or cleavage or a mixture of both in the United States, we shall analyze the values and myths they reinforce, the kinds of social problems they raise, and the blame (if any) they allocate. We shall make passing reference to some of the solutions the PSAs advocate, although this subject will be dealt with more extensively in the section on participation and passivity. Indeed, it is appropriate to point out here that there is a mild degree of discomfort, if not distortion, inherent in the way we shall discuss separate dimensions of the PSAs under different aspects of our three chapters on consensus-cleavage, instrumental-affective orientations, and participation-passivity. Nonetheless, no Procrustes we.

VALUES

Warren Breed contends that "as a form of adult socialization, the media are seen as guarantors that a bond of common ultimate values remains visible as a continuing source of consensus, despite the inroads of change. . . . Writers for years have held that the media serve certain societal and cultural purposes by bringing people into community relations and aiding their socialization into approved forms of behavior."[2]

If Breed is accurate, PSAs should be rife with values invoking cooperation as they depict and encourage interaction among the American people. Analysis of our sample determined that this is indeed the case. The largest number of PSAs in our sample, almost 30 percent, evoked humanitarianism, an additional 11 percent specifically urged viewers to cooperate with their fellows or society's institutions, 8 percent advocated brotherhood, 5 percent told viewers to be a part of society, and smaller percentages advocated such values as tolerance, patriotism, and obedience to the laws. The overwhelming majority of the values in our sample, then, provided a basis for the cooperative ethos. "Take Stock in America!" advocate the PSAs for U.S. Savings Bonds, endorsing capitalism, patriotism, and interest in one fell slogan.

A 60-second Red Cross spot is one of numerous examples of the way in which PSAs instill cooperation and trust among their viewers. A young Red Cross volunteer named Alice pedals her bicycle around a small town to visit isolated members of the community. She arrives at the home of two old ladies who are obviously delighted to see her again. Generational differences vanish as the three women converse and show great interest in each other's activities. The announcer asks what kind of person would give up her free time to do the work of the Red Cross. Clearly someone unselfish and helpful (and young and attractive). The PSA then urges the viewer to "Be a Good Neighbor" and to volunteer for the Red Cross. This advertisement, and especially its slogan, exemplifies the cooperative ethos based on concern for one's fellows that is fundamental to consensus.

Sometimes it is not the frequency of a value which is important but its pervasiveness and dominance in PSAs concerned with a particular subject. For example, the two most prevalent values in PSAs related to the American economy are productivity and employment opportunity. We discussed the former in our analysis of the government-Advertising Council productivity campaign in Chapter 2. The latter is exemplified by a National Alliance of Businessmen-Advertising Council commercial showing unemployed black youth in which we are informed that the way to get America working is to get people working; employers are asked to call the alliance if they have any jobs available. Simultaneously, in the productivity campaign, productivity is defined as a function of individual effort rather than organization, structure, and internal authority relations of American business. Coincidentally, a Department of Labor PSA tells viewers: "You Can't Get Tomorrow's Jobs with Today's Skills."

If employment opportunities are available, then we must blame ourselves, not our institutions and leaders, for our failure to advance. If productivity is a function of our individual efforts, then it becomes that much harder to blame economic decline upon our business and political leaders; even if we do blame them, it is their individual incapacities we indict, not the economic and political systems. And by accepting the value of private property implicit in these advertisements, we tacitly and perhaps unwittingly countenance the uneven distribution of wealth. The economic status quo is reinforced and the consensus undisturbed.

Roughly 30 percent of the PSAs contained values which, although also conveyed by such traditional socializing agents of society as home, school, and church, do not inevitably promote the cooperative ethos. We refer to such values as good health, safety, family life and family togetherness, self-help, temperance, capitalism, and honesty (they are in some cases mutually exclusive). It is possible that trying to maximize any one or more of these values could bring an individual into conflict with some of his fellows. Nonetheless, to the extent that any of these values promotes conflict, it does so within Almond and Verba's "higher, overarching attitudes of solidarity"—conflict within a consensus framework.

Similarly, when we classified our PSAs according to their apparent main purpose, rather than their primary value, we discovered that roughly 5 percent of them could be classified as "appreciative awareness." Such PSAs appear designed to increase viewers' awareness and appreciation of America's diversity and the opportunities it offers by extolling our natural and man-made resources, purportedly available for public use and enjoyment (for example, America's forests), or by celebrating America's ethnic diversity. In these PSAs, physical variety (geographical and human) is shown to contribute to national consensus.

Just because PSAs overwhelmingly contain values encouraging consensus, they are not inherently precluded from espousing controversial positions that might stimulate societal conflict. We therefore categorized our PSAs as noncontroversial or controversial. The former express a viewpoint about which there is general consensus in our society. A controversial PSA concerns a subject over which there is considerable disagreement in the society and which might go beyond the cleavage tolerable within the general consensus. In view of our evidence that groups espousing controversial views are virtually excluded from television, we expected very few controversial PSAs. There were none.

Some PSAs start out as if they intend to promote controversy but, in our experience, they never execute their threat. We were almost convinced by one that began by announcing "Today there's a revolution going on," and then showed girls running, playing tennis, swimming, diving, and so on. Naively we anticipated a mild endorsement of women's liberation. We were traduced by the use of the term "revolution." The admonition was to support physical fitness programs in our schools.

The only way in which any of the monitored PSAs could be defined as conflictive was if its general goal was noncontroversial but it was competing with other groups for resources (for example, appealing for funds). Even defining conflict so broadly, only 36 percent of our PSAs were conflictive—and it is certainly not political conflict. Thus, PSAs through the values they espouse and their general subject matter emphasize the consensus in the society while giving negligible visibility to cleavage and conflict.

PROBLEMS

Despite their lack of controversy, most public service announcements are about problems, even though it should be observed that there are no PSAs for a wide variety of problems, such as tennis elbow and frisbee finger, which afflict far more Americans than do many of the diseases featured in the advertisements. In effect, PSAs help set our social priorities. As our discussion of economic values suggests, PSAs could disrupt consensus and promote conflict through the specific problems they raise and the blame they allocate. The economic example indicated that such conflict-causing content is unlikely to be shown. But economics is a delicate subject from which it may be misleading to extrapolate. Do PSAs raise problems? What or whom do they blame? What kinds of solutions do they propose?

Some 37 percent of our PSA sample consisted of what we characterize as personal admonitions in which viewers are urged to take action to solve particular problems, for example, to help prevent forest fires. An additional 27 percent we define as solicitations, in which viewers are asked (implored) for funds to support medical research or to help those in distress (Muscular Dystrophy, the Kidney Foundation). These PSAs are preceded by a justification for their pleas to the viewers. This is not necessarily the case with PSAs in our other categories: for example, appreciative awareness PSAs celebrate America and refer to no problems whatsoever.

The problems featured in the personal admonition and solicitation PSAs are typically revealed through their effects on individuals (actors or nonactors) who are the subjects of the PSAs. They often concern people in unfortunate circumstances who need our help—children, foreigners, victims of natural disasters or disease.

The focus on individuals is endemic in television. It is partly a limitation of the technology and a lack of creativity, and partly a graphic device in which the person or people shown are supposed to stand for all others with similar problems. Whatever the reasons, one effect is to deemphasize or omit causal factors for the problems shown other than individual carelessness, incapacity, bad luck, affliction, or fate.

Problems are raised, and victims and sufferers depicted or described. Is any blame placed? Not often. Of all the PSAs that identified problems, 62 percent assigned no blame at all. The 38 percent that did place blame laid it on the individual (29 percent), society in general (6 percent), and business (3 percent). Not a single PSA blamed government or any public official. It appears that the government-advertising nexus that produces PSAs is able to use them to exonerate itself of responsibility for societal problems by neglecting to discuss the causes or by pointing to the individual American as the source. As a result, trust between rulers and followers is undiminished, conflict not fomented, existing societal cleavages neither highlighted nor exacerbated, and consensus enhanced.

A Keep America Beautiful PSA exemplifies this situation. The spot shows a majestic American Indian paddling a canoe down a river that becomes progressively more polluted. Factories and smokestacks are depicted at a considerable distance (two of the authors failed to notice them on initial viewing). The

Indian then comes ashore near a highway littered with refuse. At this point a bag of trash is thrown and lands at the Indian's feet. As the camera focuses on a tear running down the Indian's cheek, the slogan appears: "People Start Pollution, People Can Stop It." The slogan defines the problem as litter and the blame as individual, thereby relieving economic institutions and public officials of responsibility. Criticism of industry's role in causing pollution is deflected by emphasizing the extent to which pollution is the responsibility of individuals. The fight against pollution is equated with antilitter efforts rather than with auto emission controls, smokestack filters, or prohibitions on nonreturnable bottles and cans.

The only PSA we encountered on television, either during our monitoring period or the several years we watched less systematically, that evoked any semblance of discontent with or distrust of American institutions, was a CARE PSA showing the unfortunate conditions of some of the people in Vietnam. But the PSA itself placed no blame for the conditions depicted; it merely resurrected our antipathy to the war and our residual disgust over America's participation in it.

SOLUTIONS

Many PSAs, having shown and told viewers of societal problems, then suggest solutions. In our section on participation, we shall discuss in detail the implications and possible effects of these proposed "solutions." Since they bear on the consensus-conflict dimension, we also consider them briefly here.

The solutions to societal problems contained in PSAs are becoming informed, being concerned, and engaging in some form of individual action. A combination of these courses is sometimes encouraged. Thus the American Cancer Society appeals for a "Checkup and a Check." The actions encouraged range from the vague, leaving considerable leeway to the individual imagination, to the precise, which tries to deny discretion. PSAs exhort us to "love one another" and to "get the problem drinker off the road for his sake and yours." Both tasks are formidable, and neither PSA advises us what to do to implement the admonition or how to accomplish it. When told "Don't Be Fuelish!" we are instructed on the appropriate steps to follow and admonished that it is up to each of us.

The underlying value in these "solutions" is the optimistic American belief (not without some foundation) that diseases can be cured and problems solved—a belief in progress. The keys to progress are money and education. And the progress itself benefits all Americans; it comes from cooperation, not conflict.

Cooperation within consensus is formally encouraged in three ways. First the individual American is responsible and must act individually by turning off lights, driving slower, and not littering. The aggregation of individual actions conduces to an America self-sufficient in energy and environmentally sound. Second, the individual gives funds to institutions working to cure disease and improve the material lot of the unfortunate at home and abroad, such as CARE. Finally, a small percentage of PSAs explicitly calls for cooperative action to solve societal problems. The thrust of these PSAs is to persuade viewers to join with societal institutions, not just with each other, to solve problems in a prescribed manner. Thus individual, group, and institutional efforts combine through cooperation, not conflict, under the umbrella of shared values, to a better America.

DEPOLITICIZATION

Conflict is contagious in a democracy. It transforms private disagreements into public, and therefore political, issues. People come to see their individual stakes involved. But many private disagreements remain private, because the protagonists realize it is in their interests to keep them secluded from public view while they work out mutually beneficial or tolerable accommodations among themselves. PSAs contribute to this depoliticization of issues by helping to define them as appropriate for professional, technical, or individual solutions—anything that avoids political conflict.

Warren Breed's research led him to the conclusion that what the media neglect is just as important as what they bring to the attention of the public. As he concluded, "The media, then, withdraw from unnecessarily baring structural flaws in the working of the institutions."[3] PSAs constitute a part of the "continuing source of consensus" of which Breed writes. Through the values they espouse, the blame they fail to attribute, the blame they do attribute, the solutions to problems they propose; and by excluding dissident groups, by refusing to consider certain subjects, and by depoliticizing issues, PSAs contribute to consensus by not "baring structural flaws."

NOTES

1. Gabriel A. Almond and Sidney Verba, *The Civic Culture* (Princeton: Princeton University Press, 1963), pp. 491, 492.

2. Warren Breed, "Mass Communication and Sociocultural Integration," in *People, Society, and Mass Communications,* ed. Lewis Anthony Dexter and David Manning White (New York: The Free Press, 1964), pp. 187, 188.

3. Ibid., p. 196.

CHAPTER

10

PSAs AND INSTRUMENTAL-AFFECTIVE ORIENTATIONS

According to Almond and Verba, there must be a balance in the civic culture between instrumental and affective orientations toward the political system. The support for governmental authority stems from two sources, the citizen's diffuse emotional attachment to the system and his expectation of positive benefits to be accrued from being a member of the system. If the attachment of the citizenry is based solely on the expectation of benefits, that attachment most probably will dissolve during times when, for whatever reasons, these benefits are not forthcoming.[1] On the other hand, if the attachment is purely emotional, then the balance between passivity and participation is tipped in the direction of the latter, as citizens become deeply involved in politics. This involvement tends to "foster the sort of mass, messianic movements that lead to democratic instability." Hence, "politics must not be so instrumental and pragmatic that participants lose all emotional involvement in it. On the other hand, the level of affective orientation toward politics ought not to become too intense."[2]

DEPICTION OF AUTHORITY

PSAs could relate to Almond and Verba's instrumental and affective orientations in various ways. Most devastatingly, they could portray government and established institutions as inept and hostile to the interests of most Americans—thus leading to a decline, if not the demise, of both instrumental and affective orientations. PSAs do no such thing. Rather, they seem crafted, although not necessarily always consciously, to show public and private institutions and organizations, as well as the people occupying positions of authority in them, as both instrumentally effective and deserving of our approval and affection. We are told over and over again, for example, that the Department of

Housing and Urban Development (HUD) helps people by providing flood insurance, that HUD is for America, "A Nation of Neighbors." The Veterans Administration tells us it can help (G.I. Bill). The President's Council on Physical Fitness and Sports wants us to live longer. The Agriculture Department warns us about salmonella. Between cartoons on Saturday mornings, two black shoes inform us of the U.S. Office of Education's Basic Opportunity Grants program. A PSA on the CBS morning news advises us to contact the National Institute on Alcoholism for information and help. And around Christmas time, the marines collect Toys for Tots by PSA.

More systematically, we analyzed our PSAs to determine how often and in what ways they depicted authority. Roughly 62 percent contained no overt portrayals of politically relevant authority. PSAs do not frequently remind viewers of the existence of a political world with a hierarchy of command and control. When authority does obtrude, there seems to be a deliberate effort to conceal the existence of governmental sanctions affecting the lives of viewers.

Very rarely there appears a PSA whose content could be construed as government interfering in our lives. But such PSAs are almost invariably noncontroversial and are presented in the spirit of traditional American values. Thus a Department of Labor PSA informing viewers of their rights to additional pay if they work beyond a specified number of hours is so innocuous that only Scrooge could cavil—and he was English. We saw this PSA only once during our several years of viewing.

One might imagine that PSAs sponsored by the Internal Revenue Service would contain warnings about the sanctions for cheating, tardiness, or any of the other derelictions to which tax payers are heir. Not so. The Internal Revenue Service PSA slogan is "We Want to Help." Typically, a 1975 IRS commercial encouraged us to mail our returns early by showing comedian Sid Caesar doing just that and returning home to find his refund waiting for him. Although this is a clear case of deceptive advertising, we lack the temerity to bring it to the attention of the Federal Trade Commission.

Only antidrug PSAs clearly fail to encourage a favorable orientation among all viewers towards the instrumental and affective dimensions of government. Obviously those users devoid of guilt about their habit, and resenting antidrug laws, can hardly respond with positive affect to a government purportedly bent on depriving them of their pleasure and punishing them to boot, nor can they applaud the instrumental effectiveness of such a government. And yet, in taking on the drug culture, the government does endear itself to the vast majority of Americans who abhor drug usage (if one omits over-the-counter and legally prescribed drugs) and seek its elimination. Furthermore, the criticism antidrug efforts have encountered and the changes made in the program suggest how reluctant governmental agencies are to castigate and threaten, or at least warn, any sizable segment of the population of the sanctions for even clearly illegal behavior. Indeed, it is instructive that the PSAs we have recently seen most often deal with Americans arrested abroad for illegal use or possession of drugs. Punishment by foreign governments is stressed: "When You're Busted for Drugs Over There, You're in for the Hassle of Your Life."

We discovered three PSAs which could be construed as suggesting the possibility that the American government specifically applies sanctions to miscreants. The first, sponsored by the North Carolina Division of Wildlife (and therefore a state, not a national, PSA) advised viewers of the turkey-shooting season and the limit on the number of birds that could be bagged. Implicit in the PSA was a sanction for hunting out of season or killing more than the maximum. But these aspects were submerged in the primary message encouraging North Carolinians to enjoy the opportunity to hunt.

The second PSA, sponsored by the Department of Transportation via the Advertising Council, features what we take to be a state policeman (so convincing he is probably an actor) who instructs viewers that the 55-mile-per-hour speed limit is "not just a good idea, it's the law." This recent addition to the PSA galaxy is conspicuous for its stern tone and vigorous endorsement of a national law. We suspect it represents an aberration rather than a trend. Besides, people are no doubt aware that the maximum speed limit is often violated by drivers and unenforced by the police.

Only one PSA both specifically imposed a legal obligation on viewers and warned of severe penalties for failure to comply. This was a message appearing during January telling foreigners resident as immigrants in the United States of the impending registration deadline. In the world of public service advertising, only aliens are threatened drastically by U.S. governmental sanctions.

Some 38 percent of our PSAs contained authority figures—doctors, nurses, parents, military personnel, and policemen. Almost invariably they were depicted as competent, helpful, and benevolent in carrying out their duties. For example, a PSA sponsored by the American Automobile Association's Foundation for Traffic Safety starts by showing two inebriated men in a bar "having one more for the road." When they leave the bar, the driver assures his friend that he can drive, at which point his friend passes out. The next scene shows their car running off the road; it ends up perched on the edge of a cliff. A policeman arrives promptly at the scene and politely and deferentially asks the driver how the accident occurred. The driver asserts his sobriety and to prove it opens the door; he falls off the edge of the cliff (hurting mainly his vanity we gather), while the announcer intones, "Sure, buddy, sure." The PSA is typical in placing responsibility for undesirable social occurrences (in this case traffic accidents) on the individual rather than, say, on inadequate highway design or the faulty construction of automobiles. The officer's prompt arrival at the accident scene, the patience and understanding of his questions, and his sober image contrasted with the driver's drunken ineptitude, depict the police force as competent, helpful, and trustworthy, and thus tend to reinforce the authority vested in the police.

Not only are governmental authority in general and the individuals who execute it presented favorably in PSAs, but governmental and allied private agencies emerge as solicitous, concerned, expert, efficient, and benevolent. Indeed, whenever a PSA had occasion to depict an institution such as a hospital, school, or nursing home, the institution appeared to be immaculate, possessed of all the newest facilities, and staffed by personnel who seemed concerned for those in their charge. Never was it implied that the institution and its personnel were anything less than fully competent to deal with the problems they faced.

To avid viewers of public service advertisements like us, PSAs often seem to be nothing more than gallant and not entirely unsuccessful attempts by Washington bureaucrats to counter the contumely to which they are sometimes subjected by members of the American public. One reason is obvious: these agencies sponsor the PSAs. But there are more subtle explanations having to do with the general approach of the PSAs and the nature of their appeals.

OTHER APPEALS

In analyzing our PSAs, we categorized roughly 37 percent as "personal admonitions." These warn viewers of the consequences of such actions as drunken driving, improper use of pesticides, smoking, and so on. They urge the individual to take action to correct such behavior. They implicitly uphold the authority of the sponsoring institution by implying that adverse consequences will occur if the viewer does not comply with the messages–consequences which will be self-inflicted and the viewer's own fault, not a result of governmental action. The sponsoring agency, moreover, appears efficient, helpful, and concerned about the welfare of Americans while, within the PSA, violators are depicted unfavorably.

An additional 12 percent of our PSAs fall into the category of "services available," informing viewers of help provided through the auspices of government and nonprofit organizations–for example, a state employment agency notifies viewers about available jobs. They obviously appeal to viewers' instrumental orientations by emphasizing the productive activities of societal institutions and the benefits they provide.

Other categories of PSAs, such as "societal admonitions," which call for viewers to cooperate with government or other institutions in the solution of social problems, and "appreciative awareness" (previously discussed under consensus) paeans to the glories of America's human and natural resources, obviously reinforce instrumental and affective orientations. Similarly, the recruitment and solicitation PSAs, 15 and 27 percent respectively of our sample, encourage these feelings and beliefs. Recruitment appeals either show government and nonprofit agencies as caring about and trying to help deserving people in America and abroad or feature an efficient and capable military service deserving public support. Solicitations generally emphasize progress in the fight against debilitating diseases and depict the soliciting agency as efficient and effective. We shall discuss these kinds of PSAs at greater length in our chapter on participation.

The nature of the appeals contained in PSAs also contributes to reinforcing viewers' instrumental confidence in and positive feelings for American governmental and public-oriented private institutions. In trying to persuade viewers, most PSAs contain appeals either to rational pragmatism or to the emotions or, frequently, both. Almost half of the PSAs appealed to the viewers' self-interest by referring to the benefits to be gained by complying with the message. The emotions most often evoked were altruism and sympathy and were thus directed at evoking positive affect towards both one's fellow citizens and the sponsor of the message—often a governmental agency. PSAs also balance a pragmatic, goal-oriented approach to government with a diffuse emotional attachment to the government and society as a whole. There are PSAs which appeal to such sentiments as patriotism and trust in authority figures and a similar proportion which appeal to pragmatic self-interest by pointing out the congruence of the goals of authority figures with the wishes of viewers.

One final way in which PSAs contribute to enhancing both the instrumental and affective dimensions of their governmental and nongovernmental sponsors is through the process of status conferral. This occurs in two parts: through sponsorship and through the sources of authority appealed to in the PSAs themselves.

Individuals and organizations gain status and even legitimacy by appearing in the media and especially on television. If they were not somehow deserving, why would they appear when other individuals and organizations are denied access? Television appearances are not necessarily unalloyed blessings; one can be portrayed as foolish, incompetent, or venal. The sponsors of PSAs, however, are able to avoid most of the impediments to status conferral and exploit all the opportunities. They have control over their messages, which are not edited, interfered with, or commented upon by television personnel. The messages are designed to portray the sponsoring agency favorably and to show it as caring, effective, and deserving of public support. Only in their lack of substantial control over the decisions at local stations whether and when to show PSAs are the sponsors limited in enhancing their status.

THE PURPOSE OF PSAs

This raises an interesting question concerning the purpose of PSAs. If our sample is indeed representative, then a relatively large portion of PSAs are concerned with obtaining the viewer's support for such organizations as the American Cancer Society, the Arthritis Foundation, and the Red Cross. These PSAs would seem to be oriented more towards ensuring the continued existence of these organizations than towards providing the viewer with any benefit. Some PSAs, indeed, go even further and either indirectly or directly advertise services or products. These include exhortations to seek regular dental care and have medical checkups—a form of promotion for dentists and doctors—and PSAs informing us about vitamins (from Miles Laboratories), or a message from the makers of Pepsi Cola (clearly identified), or an advertisement for hearing aids.

There are even times when the primary purpose of a PSA is to enhance the sponsor's status. Thus, the Liggett Group (formerly Liggett and Myers, Inc.) buys several million dollars worth of television time to promote its Alpo dog food, Blue Lustre cleaning product, National Oats, and Brite watchbands. It also produces several liquor products such as J&B Scotch and Wild Turkey bourbon which cannot be advertised on television and radio. The largest part of its business, cigarettes, similarly is banned from the broadcast media. Using such well-known pop singers as Bette Midler and Jay and the Americans, the Liggett Group reportedly spent some $250,000 to produce and distribute a series of one-minute PSAs for America's bicentennial. They were "filled with 'group spirit' in their depiction of various groups of Americans living together in peace and harmony."[3] According to company president Raymond J. Mulligan, their primary objective is "to enhance the identity of our new corporate trademark. . . and to associate it with upscale prestigious public service messages related to the Bicentennial celebration."[4]

Sponsor status is further enhanced by the authoritative sources and data cited by PSAs to support their arguments. Such material justifies the sponsor's position, and thus his credibility and legitimacy. Almost a quarter of our sample used empirical illustrations; for example, a dramatic illustration in a drunk driving PSA showing a man drinking excessively and then being involved in an automobile accident. Almost another 25 percent relied upon sponsors' expertise, with the sponsor shown to be knowledgeable and experienced in dealing with the problem. Other authoritative sources invoked were history (2 percent)—a recruitment PSA referring to the glorious tradition of the marines; statistics (5 percent)—the number of deaths caused by drunk drivers cited in a drunk driving PSA; personal experience (5 percent)—testimony from people who have personally experienced the problems depicted; personal expertise (2 percent)—the appearance of a doctor in an antismoking spot discussing cancer; and government (2 percent)—government agencies or persons within government specifically referred to in the PSA, for example, erstwhile President Nixon's firm antidrug posture cited in a drug abuse spot.

PSAs are a force for increasing the degree of satisfaction with and support of the political system because of the opportunities they afford governmental agencies and established nongovernmental institutions to display themselves as active, concerned, beneficent—in a word, as responsive to the needs of the American people. There are reasons for deploring such an outcome. First, the private organizations that sponsor PSAs may not deserve our support. The most reputable organization, when scrutinized, can be discovered to be rife with fundamental weaknesses.[5] Even the Red Cross, whose PSAs appear frequently on the airwaves, has been found in a study by independent consultants to have "poor planning and ignorance in its ranks," as well as "'a lack of will to improve.'"[6]

More significantly, consider the example of the American Bar Association. Its local affiliates sponsor occasional public service announcements in which they appear to advocate legal services for all. Yet the depth of the ABA's concern for widespread, inexpensive legal services can be questioned. It has vigorously opposed group legal programs and advertising and soliciting by lawyers that could reduce legal costs, while adamantly supporting minimum fee schedules that have kept legal costs high. Such "routine tasks as uncontested divorces, title searches, simple wills and bankruptcies" could be handled by paralegals with substantial reductions of fees and "small-claims courts, computer facilities, no-fault compensation and arbitration boards can provide low-cost justice in many situations."[7] The organized bar has been less than enthusiastic in pursuing such cost-reducing opportunities.

The ABA is not alone in its vulnerability to criticism. Many of the sponsors of PSAs may acquire and distribute money for formal education (United Negro College Fund) or health research (American Cancer Society), but they do it in ways that perpetuate existing structures and processes–structures and processes which may not adequately be serving their manifest purposes, which may need overhauling or scrapping. As Amitai Etzioni argues: "One essential lesson of the last decades has been that universities, corporations, labor unions, hospitals, and school systems have all been politicized and recognized as 'private' governments and institutions in which one must participate if one wishes to share in the business of societal guidance."[8] PSAs display these institutions as capable, competent, beneficent, and expert, and stress their nonpolitical quality. Consequently, these instituitions have their autonomy enhanced and their lack of public accountability perpetuated.

The second reason for deploring the effect of PSAs in increasing the degree of support for the instrumental and affective dimensions of government is that they may be contributing to making the government less salient. Stanley Allen Renshon proposes three conditions that may cause the political system to become salient to the individual. Two are of particular interest here. In the first, the political system "may be seen as the only source capable of supplying certain benefits in the form of either goods or services"[9] PSAs do, as we have pointed out, show the government as providing goods and services which viewers are urged to use, but benefits are also depicted coming from numerous semiprivate, private, and charitable organizations. Renshon's second condition making the political system salient to the individual occurs if "the decisional outputs of the political system may be viewed as interfering with the pursuit of an individual's values and goals."[10] PSAs rarely, if ever, portray government in this way; if they do, it is only in terms of a higher, more treasured American value.

That PSAs portraying governmental agencies so attractively may be making an impression is suggested by a survey conducted by the University of Michigan's Institute for Social Research. "Three out of four persons thought that 'most of the people who work for government offices work hard and try to do a good job.' " More significantly, the researchers "were surprised to find that people who had good experiences with government agencies rated the quality of public offices no better than people who had no experience at all."[11]

The conflict between instrumental and affective orientations which so concerns Almond and Verba is muted by PSAs. Why? Because PSAs reinforce both. They show government and allied institutions as both instrumentally effective *and* deserving of affect. Because PSAs inspire such trust and promote the legitimacy of established governmental and private institutions, they provide discretionary power for political and business elites. As Almond and Verba put it in a far more benign context: "The sense of trust in the political elite—the belief that they are not alien and extractive forces but part of the same political community—makes citizens willing to turn power over to them."[12] But the citizens' trust may not be justified.

NOTES

1. Gabriel A. Almond and Sidney Verba, *The Civic Culture* (Princeton: Princeton University Press, 1963), p. 488.

2. Ibid.

3. "Liggett Image Spots Pushed as Pubservice," *Variety*, February 26, 1975.

4. Ibid.

5. For a survey and discussion of the intricacies of the charity process and the considerable variation in the honesty, efficiency, and effectiveness of assorted charitable organizations, see Harvey Katz, *Give! Who Gets Your Charity Dollar* (New York: Doubleday-Anchor, 1974).

6. "Red Cross Called Troubled Agency," New York *Times*, October 12, 1975, p. 19.

7. Mark J. Green, "The High Cost of Lawyers," *New York Times Magazine*, August 10, 1975, p. 57.

8. Amitai Etzioni, review of Sidney Verba and Norman H. Nie, *Participation In America* (New York: Harper and Row, 1972), in *Public Opinion Quarterly* 37 (1973-74): 660.

9. Stanley Allen Renshon, *Psychological Needs and Political Behavior* (New York: The Free Press, 1974), p. 76.

10. Ibid.

11. Institute for Social Research, University of Michigan, *Newsletter* 1, no. 20 (Winter 1974): 3, 6.

12. Almond and Verba, *Civic Culture*, p. 490.

CHAPTER

11

PSAs AND POLITICAL PARTICIPATION

Lester Milbrath has observed that "as long as public officials perform their tasks well, most citizens seem content not to become involved in politics."[1] PSAs contribute to this lack of political involvement both by their presentation of consensus as against conflict, and by their depictions of governmental and allied institutions as instrumentally effective and worthy of approbation. As we have documented, public officials are shown as caring, efficient, and acting in harmony with traditional American values. The impression is conveyed that they perform their tasks well, even though this may often not be the case—of course it is the impression of official competence, not the actuality, which determines public response.

Yet probably the most significant effect PSAs have on the political system is their contribution to the participation-passivity balance. For the balance between citizen participation and citizen passivity is, we believe, the most important of Almond and Verba's three balances and is central to their analysis of the civic culture. It exposes an apparently crucial contradiction in democratic theory. If elites are to be responsive, ordinary citizens must express their opinions, be involved in politics, and be influential. But, "if elites are to be powerful and make authoritative decisions, then the involvement, activity, and influence of the ordinary man must be limited. The ordinary citizen must turn power over to elites and let them rule. The need for elite power requires that the ordinary citizen be relatively passive, uninvolved, and deferential to elites."[2]

THEORIES OF PARTICIPATION

According to Almond and Verba, this apparent contradiction between the need for effective power by elites, on the one hand, and their responsiveness to the citizenry, on the other, is primarily resolved through the existence of two gaps (they seem more like chasms to us). The first gap is between the high perception by many Americans of their potential political influence and the far lower level of their actual influence. As Almond and Verba put it, "Only a small proportion of those respondents who say they could influence the government report that they have ever attempted such influence. And even if those who think they could influence governmental decisions were to attempt to do so—which is unlikely—they would almost certainly not have the success that they believe they would have."[3] The second gap exists between the "high frequency of expressed obligation to participate and the actual importance and amount of participation."[4] That is, far more citizens say that they and their compatriots have an obligation to participate than actually do participate.

Almond and Verba conclude that the citizen's role "as an active and influential enforcer of the responsiveness of elites is maintained by his strong commitment to the norms of active citizenship, as well as by his perception that he can be an influential citizen."[5] They concede that this is at least in part a myth, but argue that citizens in the civic culture with this sense of political competence have a reserve of influence—a potential to act if necessary. They thus refer to him or her as "the potentially active citizen."[6]

The gap between the political norms and perceptions held by Americans and their actual political behavior is concealed most of the time because these potentially active citizens are infrequently activated. "Because politics has little importance for them, few citizens are motivated to think about their influence or their political activities."[7] Nonetheless, issues intense enough to provoke some citizens to participate in politics do sometimes arise. The participation is usually followed by reaction from the rulers and concomitant relaxation by citizens. Almond and Verba dub these "cycles of citizen involvement, elite response, and citizen withdrawal."[8]

Finally, balance between participation and passivity is maintained, claim Almond and Verba, by the distribution of attitudes among the population: "Some individuals believe that they are competent and some do not; some individuals are active and some are not."[9]

In 1972, Sidney Verba and Norman H. Nie published *Participation in America,*[10] which takes a somewhat different view of political participation from that contained in *The Civic Culture.* Instead of the stability of democracy, their concern is with the relationship between participation and the government's allocation of resources and benefits. They distinguish four modes of participation: voting, campaign activity, cooperative activity (such as people joining together to support a bond issue), and citizen-initated contacts of public officials.[11] Within these modes they identify what they call "the six most difficult acts."[12] These are contacting a local official, attending a rally, contacting a state or national official, forming a group, giving money, and being a member of a political organization. Six percent of the population claim to have participated in four or more of these activities.[13] Indeed, the only activity in which a majority of their respondents claim to engage in regularly is voting in presidential elections.[14] Even more important, Verba and Nie reveal that the Americans who participate most are disproportionately drawn from "those with higher income, higher education, and higher status occupations."[15] And of most significance for our discussion, the government is more responsive to such people—"participation helps those who are already better off."[16]

Verba and Nie's data convince us that the participation-passivity balance endorsed in *The Civic Culture* mainly benefits the elite who rule and the minority who participate in politics—both disproportionately people with high incomes, high education, and high status. Almond and Verba may have acted in error, or at least too hastily, in rejecting the rationality-activist model of democracy just because citizens in a democracy rarely live up to it. Similarly, Verba and Nie do little to explain the interrelationship of cultural, psychological, and structural causes of this apparent unwillingness and inability of the mass public to participate extensively in politics. Carole Pateman trenchantly criticizes their failure to "consider whether their findings might not support the argument that the realization of the central democratic values requires a participatory society."[17]

Pateman's argument, elaborated in her *Participation and Democratic Theory,* is an attempt to rebut what she characterizes as the contemporary theory of democracy. In this theory, democracy

> refers to a political method or set of institutional arrangements at national levels. The characteristically democratic element in the method is the competition of leaders (elites) for the votes of the people at periodic, free elections. . . . Responsiveness of leaders to non-elite demands, or "control" over leaders is ensured primarily through the sanction of loss of office at elections; the decisions of leaders can also be influenced by active groups bringing pressure to bear during inter-election periods. "Political equality" in the theory refers to universal suffrage and to the existence of equality of opportunity of access to channels of influence over leaders. Finally, "participation," so far as the majority is concerned, is participation in the choice of decision makers.[18]

This so-called contemporary theory of democracy is suspiciously redolent of the civic culture of Almond and Verba. Opposed to it is a model drawn from Rousseau, John Stuart Mill, and G.D.H. Cole, expanded and expounded by Pateman. The individual citizen participates in making decisions. Such participation begets more participation and an appreciation of democracy, as practice makes perfect. Such a participatory society requires the diffusion of democracy and equality throughout the institutions of society in nongovernmental authority structures, especially in industry. "Specifically, the development of a sense of political efficacy does appear to depend on whether this work situation allows him any scope to participate in decision making."[19] In sum,

> the argument of the participatory theory of democracy is that participation in the alternative areas would enable the individual better to

> appreciate the connection between the public and the private spheres. The ordinary man might still be more interested in things nearer home, but the existence of a participatory society would mean that he was better able to assess the performance of representatives at the national level, better equipped to take decisions of national scope when the opportunity arose to do so, and better able to weigh up the impact of decisions taken by national representatives on his own life and immediate surroundings.[20]

Real participation, then, means participation in decision making. It means the possession of at least some degree of control over decisions, and adequate information on which to base them. Participation thus defined must be distinguished from pseudo-participation in which individuals are led to accept and endorse decisions already made. In such pseudo-participation situations, authority figures who are neither selected by nor responsible to those below for their actions try to create feelings or illusions of participation through discussion.[21] The result is participation of style not substance, in which manipulation is substituted for coercion.

The leading books on the causes and nature of political participation pay little attention to the mass media except to try to relate the amount of media consumption to the level and nature of participation. Such neglect is understandable and deplorable. It is understandable because the impact of the media—typified, we would argue, by PSAs—is difficult to discern. Media effects are often a function of ostensibly entertaining content, rather than public affairs and news programs—of what is not shown, more than what is shown. It is necessary, moreover, to analyze not just the media's explicit messages and significant omissions, but the underlying content: status conferral, values, and images of authority.

The neglect is deplorable because it perpetuates the disregard of the environmental and agenda-setting functions of the media; it ignores the media's crucial activating potential. We agree with James Rosenau that "for most active citizens there is an activator—another citizen, an organization, or a public official who evokes the behavior that we call participation through an appeal for support."[22] The media can activate or deactivate political participation.

The significance of the media looms when we consider the variables Rosenau identifies as related to participation and, specifically, to the differences among ordinary, attentive, and mobilizable citizens (the ones most likely to participate in politics). Among the salient variables Rosenau mentions are the participator's social background, "sense of efficacy, his level of information, his degree of satisfaction with the political system, his personality, his organizational memberships, his attitudes towards issues, his community's norms with respect to the appropriateness of being politically active. . . . "[23] In analyzing public service advertisements, we have argued that they bear on all these variables except social background and personality. We want now to extend and amplify our analysis.

Do PSAs encourage political participation or passivity? If they encourage participation, does it lead to the contemporary theory of democracy with its constrained conception of political activity, or does it conduce to the participatory theory of democracy elaborated by Pateman? What are the relationships between PSAs and the apparent contradiction in the civic culture between the supposed need for effective power by elites versus their required responsiveness to citizens? More specifically, do PSAs help perpetuate the myth of citizen influence by encouraging people to believe they possess such influence while simultaneously inhibiting them from trying to exercise it, and thus discovering they are not influential? Do PSAs activate or deactivate political participation? In answering these questions, we shall tie PSAs to the low and limited political participation of most Americans documented by Rosenau and by Verba and Nie.

PSEUDO-PARTICIPATION

As we discussed previously, PSAs show and tell viewers about societal problems. But PSAs rarely depict a problem as insoluble, no doubt because of the fundamental American myth of continuous progress through the combined resources and efforts of our society and its individual members. Indeed, our data reveal that only 7.4 percent of our PSAs offered no solution. More intriguing, all the rest urged individuals to act to solve societal problems. Not one called upon government. The emphasis, therefore, would seem to be upon the participant side of the participant-passivity dichotomy. Such a conclusion would be misleading.

The only explicitly political activity in which viewers are sometimes encouraged to participate by PSAs is voting. Such exhortations occur around presidential elections (the general elections, not primaries) and therefore were not found in our sample. They are carefully nonpartisan and simply urge viewers to register, "to go out and help someone vote," or to vote for the party of their choice. Of course, the parties of the choice of some Americans are not on the ballot; and for many others the candidates are indistinguishable and unappealing. Nonetheless, such PSAs contribute additional respectability to the one political activity in which, at least at the presidential level, a majority of Americans usually engage. The vote has been described as "a blunt instrument, and the citizen can choose neither when it is to be used, nor for whom or on what issues voting is to take place."[24] And elections may often properly be described as rituals which do little more than make legitimate elite control of the political and economic systems.

What of the other forms of participation encouraged by PSAs? Milbrath breaks down his hierarchy of political involvement into four categories: gladiatorial, transitional, spectator, and apathetic. Gladiatorial activities require considerable time, energy, and personal commitment and range from holding public or party office down to contributing time in a political campaign. The top transitional activity is attending a political meeting or rally. It is followed by making a monetary contribution to a party or candidate, and contacting a public official or political leader. Spectator activities are wearing a button or putting a sticker on the car, attempting to convince another to vote in a certain way, initiating a political discussion, voting, and exposing oneself to political stimuli (an unfortunate choice of words). Apathetics are the fourth category in the hierarchy.[25] To Milbrath's categories we would add forms of participation more challenging to the political system, such as initiating legal action, engaging in physical confrontation, and breaking the law openly or covertly.

There are primarily three kinds of "solutions" to societal problems which appear either singly or in combination in PSAs and are relevant to our discussion of political participation. These are solicitations for support, recruitment, and personal admonitions.

Solicitations for support ask viewers for funds or, much less frequently, some other help, such as volunteering time for charitable activities. Thus, during the UCLA-Ohio State football game of October 4, 1975, viewers were treated to the sight of two babies, one happy and gurgling, one sad and bawling. The moral: "Give to the college of your choice or else there may be no more colleges." More than a quarter of our sample of PSAs, roughly 27 percent, fell into the solicitation category.

Recruitment PSAs attempt to persuade viewers to volunteer for service in organizations such as the military, the Peace Corps, or VISTA. The only time we heard a reference to "leaders" was in a recruitment PSA—"The Girl Scouts Need Leaders." Recruitment PSAs composed 15.1 percent of our sample.

Personal admonitions, which constitute approximately 37 percent of our PSA, are of three kinds. First are vague exhortations—actor Robert Young as Dr. Marcus Welby urges us to get to know our local hospital; our Lung Association tells us that alert citizen action can reverse air pollution; the American Bar Association instructs us to support court improvements (which appears to mean more judges and more work for lawyers). Second are suggestions that viewers obtain information about problems from government or private agencies. Third, are specific courses of action—the Mormon church (Jesus Christ of Latter-Day Saints) instructs us to spend time with our children (presumably building a tree house as does the father in the PSA); our Lung Association shows us the joys of joining a car pool and urges us to do so; and the Department of Transportation tells us to fasten our seat belts. We are also told to stop smoking and to stop others' smoking. These three kinds of personal admonitions are united by their focus upon individual activities as the way to solve or at least alleviate the problems depicted.

Two of Milbrath's transitional activities are making a monetary contribution to a party or candidate, and contacting a public official or political leader. Superficially, PSAs encourage viewers to engage in political actions. But as defined by the PSAs, these activities lose their political character. The appeals for money emanate from charitable organizations whose missions in most cases are explicitly humanitarian. Donations are not requested for political parties or candidates, or for advocates of policy stands that might be divisive. Rather, funds are solicited for research to produce cures for physical diseases. Indeed, the only appeals for funds for overt political activity are from such organizations as Radio Free Europe, whose endeavors, it should be noted, are directed abroad, and whose purposes were, at least until recently, noncontroversial within the United States.

Similarly, as conceived by Milbrath, contacting a public official is generally self-initiated, and the messages frequently consist of expressions of outrage, the making of demands or avowals of support. In contrast, the PSAs, by channeling a need or interest, evoke responses which, in turn, are most often requests for information offered by the sponsoring agency. The agency thus determines and structures the individual's action.

Milbrath refers to making monetary contributions and contacting public officials as transitional activities because they lead from spectator to gladiatorial behavior. "As a person becomes more involved in politics, he engages in a wider repertoire of political acts and moves upward in the hierarchy from the more frequent to the less frequent behaviors."[26] In Milbrath's formulation, contributing and contacting produce involvement with public officials and issues, the making of claims, assumptions of accountability, and responsiveness. As treated by PSAs, however, contributions and contacting are more likely to deflect from than lead to higher forms of political participation. Charitable organizations may characterize themselves as "Your" Lung or Heart Association, but they stand aloof and relatively immune from public scrutiny. The PSAs encourage the average viewer to donate but not to join or play any meaningful part in the organization's affairs. Money without interference might be their motto. Nor do the information packets provided by agencies in response to viewers' requests involve the latter in more than a client, even supplicant, relationship with public officials.

This kind of involvement deters participation by denying access. Viewers who donate, who write to governmental agencies for information, are not expressing policy preferences in a way that will be acted upon by government. They are not establishing meaningful two-way communication. They are not ensuring that policy makers will make decisions consistent with their preferences—if indeed the viewers' actions actually do indicate any preferences other than generalized support for and interest in the sponsor's activities. And they are not developing the personal skills or resources conducive to future participation.

PSAs encourage pseudo-participation by exhorting Americans to act in a limited and predetermined manner. Defining both the problems and the solutions, PSAs also define the methods by which the solutions are to be achieved. PSAs urge viewers to work within existing societal institutions, through methods of which the leaders of these institutions approve. Unconventional, let alone radical, methods are never mentioned. Moreover, the responses urged by PSAs are, in the main, relatively easy and undemanding to make (although in some cases they may result in subsequent hardship—for example, for people who join the armed services). PSAs thus divert energy and alleviate potential interest which might otherwise conduce to political activity. They provide a sense of vicarious influence, almost certainly for those who respond to them and possibly for viewers who see them but do not act. Through PSAs, viewers' high perceptions of their potential influence are reinforced while they are deterred from participating in politics in ways which would expose the insignificant amount of political influence they actually wield. Similarly, PSAs help conceal the gap between the individual's sense of obligation to participate in political life and actual minimal participation. Consequently, public service advertising helps perpetuate the myth of individual influence, the illusion of individual political competence, central to elite dominance and control.

Public service advertisements use the full panoply of persuasive techniques on behalf of the siren of pseudo-participation. They do so by implicitly and explicitly denying the need for meaningful and active individual and group participation in the institutions that dominate our everyday lives; by reinforcing the nonpartisanship norm prevalent in so many American communities; and by promoting the delusion that social and economic problems should be dealt with apolitically—that is, without resort to unbecoming political activity, conflict, and controversy. We must question whether such advertising is indeed a public service, or whether it may more appropriately be characterized as propaganda contributing to the perpetuation and support of existing social and economic relations within an arid political stability in the United States.

NOTES

1. Lester W. Milbrath, *Political Participation* (Chicago: Rand McNally, 1965), p. 143.
2. Gabriel A. Almond and Sidney Verba, *The Civic Culture* (Princeton: Princeton University Press, 1963), p. 478.
3. Ibid., p. 480.
4. Ibid., p. 481.
5. Ibid.
6. Ibid.
7. Ibid., p. 483.
8. Ibid., p. 484.
9. Ibid., p. 485.
10. Sidney Verba and Norman H. Nie, *Participation in America* (New York: Harper and Row, 1972).
11. Ibid., pp. 44-55.
12. Ibid., p. 36.
13. Ibid., p. 40.
14. Ibid., p. 31.
15. Ibid., p. 12.
16. Ibid., p. 338.

17. Carole Pateman, "To them that hath, shall be given: On 'Participation in America: Political Democracy and Social Equality' by Sidney Verba and Norman H. Nie," *Politics* (the Australasian Political Studies Association journal) 9 (November 1974): 140.

18. Carole Pateman, *Participation and Democratic Theory* (London: Cambridge University Press, 1970), p. 14.

19. Ibid., p. 53.

20. Ibid., p. 110.

21. Sidney Verba discusses pseudo-democracy in *Small Groups and Political Behavior* (Princeton: Princeton University Press, 1960), pp. 219-21. For a summary see Pateman, *Participation and Democratic Theory*, p. 69.

22. James N. Rosenau, *Citizenship Between Elections* (New York: The Free Press, 1974), p. xxix.

23. Ibid.

24. Pateman, "To them that hath," p. 143.

25. Milbrath, *Political Participation*, chap. 1 and passim.

26. Ibid., pp. 20-21.

CHAPTER

12

INCLUDING THE EXCLUDED

A public issue can arise over the distribution, redistribution, or regulation of resources and statuses within a community. As Rosenau puts it: "The core of a public issue is the debate about the priorities attached to values and their allocation, and the processes through which the debate is conducted and the values allocated may be crucial determinants of attentive and mobilized behavior."[1] We contend that public service advertisements tend either to inhibit societal problems from emerging as political issues or, if the issues have arisen and are salient to viewers, to encourage their depoliticization. PSAs concentrate attention upon the supposed incapacities and weaknesses of individuals. In so doing, they divert attention from the inadequacies of governmental programs and the pathologies of the social and economic systems. Yet, as Murray Edelman has observed, "many . . . studies suggest that the various social problems treated separately are largely symptoms of the same problem: an economic system that produces too few jobs, too little income or security and too few opportunities for self-fulfillment."[2]

America's problems could be presented to the public in ways which would raise such questions and foment divisiveness and conflict. For example, PSAs could emphasize differences in rank and challenge the legitimacy of the existing allocation of goods and services and the differential burden of costs. They could point out that some people enjoy far better material lives and greater political power than others, that equal opportunity is an American myth. Institutional racism, conflict theory, and their components of coercion and violence could be used to explain social stratification and racial discrimination.[3] In contrast to their present content, PSAs might be devised to reduce positive affect (by showing the government to be in cahoots with business and disdainful of the needs and interests of average Americans); to reduce instrumental credibility (by showing the government as ineffectual and bureaucratic); and to encourage political participation. In brief, PSAs could perhaps be devised to promote "a crisis of ideological credibility and a challenge of institutional control mechanisms in the society."[4]

Less flamboyantly, PSAs might redefine or extend the concept of charity and solicit funds for public service law firms. Implicit in such a redefinition would be the realization that societal ills are a function of social, economic, and political organization and activities and can be fought institutionally through such law firms. PSAs might both inform viewers of their rights under the law *and* encourage the assertion of such rights, especially vis-à-vis the police.

Finally, PSAs could be designed specifically to stimulate political participation. This could be achieved indirectly by the encouragement of ethnic solidarity and group consciousness (Verba and Nie found that group consciousness among blacks increased their participation and was virtually the only factor reducing the participation disparity between socioeconomic status groups).[5] PSAs could also encourage political participation directly. They might not only request charitable donations for educational institutions, medical research, and so on, but urge viewers to demand that the government provide more funds to these organizations. Viewers could be encouraged to join a political party (not confined to the Republicans or Democrats), or form a new one; to join a politically alert interest group, or to organize a new one; to invoke their rights of freedom of speech, press, assembly, and petition through teach-ins, rallies, protest marches, picketing, boycotts, and strikes; and to engage in less conventional behavior by testing the limits of civil disobedience. These are all forms of political expression and action which public service advertisements shun.

REASONS FOR EXCLUSION

We have previously chronicled at some length the exclusion from the PSA nexus of activist groups critical of established governmental and private institutions. We have documented that not only are such groups excluded, but so are their messages—messages which could encourage political perspectives and activities. Dissident groups lack the knowledge and resources to make and distribute PSAs. Should some group possess the wherewithal, the Advertising Council shields the television and radio industry from them, delaying, obfuscating, and ultimately rejecting the group's appeals for help. Finally, if the group produces PSAs and sends them of its own volition and at its own risk to local stations, they are highly unlikely to appear. With numerous PSAs from which to choose, local station gatekeepers opt for what they take to be safe, sane, and noncontroversial.

The television networks do not have policies of explicitly excluding PSAs from any nonprofit source from the airwaves. As one network official told us emphatically, "Just because an organization is controversial doesn't mean that its public service announcements will be excluded." Rather, the networks are concerned with content. Their position is most explicitly stated and perhaps best exemplified by NBC:

> Under long-standing NBC policy, uniformly applied to each PSA submission, regardless of sponsor, free public service time is not given for discussion of points of view on sectarian, political, or "controversial" issues within the meaning of the FCC rules on these subjects. We believe that the discussion of controversial political and social issues of public importance is better presented in regularly-scheduled and special NBC news and public affairs programs where such issues can be developed in a more balanced and informative manner.[6]

For the networks, information is acceptable in PSAs, points of view are not. To us, the distinction is dubious, if not moot.

Only recently have the television networks and local stations been asked to examine, let alone defend, their policy or practice of showing only what they believe to be consensual, innocuous PSAs. The network personnel responsible for airing PSAs blame the Federal Communications Commission's fairness doctrine for at least part of their caution. They assert that if they broadcast PSAs with a scent of controversy, they become vulnerable to a fairness doctrine complaint. Such complaints demanding equal time are handled by the FCC on a case-by-case basis with concomitant time and money costs to the network—costs which climb if the FCC's decision is appealed to the federal courts. No wonder PSAs which explicitly advocate are excluded. Even PSAs that simply offer the viewers a place to go for information are regarded with suspicion, especially if they emanate from anything other than an eminently respectable source. Such sponsors, too, sometimes cause problems. For example, one network showed a Sierra Club PSA reportedly containing the phrase "America's being paved over." Complaints were received from politicians and business executives critical of the assertion and challenging its statistics. Since that episode, the network involved asks that it be provided with documentation for claims made in PSAs.

For busy, harassed television executives, public service advertisements may be viewed as part of the network's or stations's contribution to the welfare of the community, but they are also an additional burden among myriad duties and responsibilities. PSAs, then, are treated with care and facility. Handling each PSA consumes time, work, and therefore money, even if no more is entailed than ensuring that clearances have been obtained from people appearing in the advertisements. But even seemingly innocuous PSAs can generate complaints, as one network found when antismoking messages were objected to on the grounds that they told children nasty things about their parents.

Beyond the fairness doctrine invoked by network and local television station executives, beyond the burdens that controversy imposes on their time and energy, lurk more substantial reasons for avoiding provocative PSAs. Such

PSAs could antagonize sponsors and offend or alienate some members of the viewing audience. One possible result would be withdrawal of advertising and a concomitant decline in profit. Another likely result would be a rash of demands for air time from offended groups to respond to the offensive PSA. As one network executive put it, "If we show a pro-abortion PSA we'll have the rest on our necks." And although the networks might be able to bear them, such pressures would be particularly hard on individual local stations fearful of antagonizing their sponsors and viewers and economically vulnerable to community outrage. And, as we discussed in Chapter 5, the United States Supreme Court has upheld the networks' right to refuse "idea" advertising for which the sponsor is willing to pay.

In view of the preceding analysis, the prospects for provocative PSAs appearing on our television screens seem remote. Public service advertising is narrowly defined by decision makers in the television industry and consists primarily of requests for charitable contributions from ostensibly reputable organizations, recruitment appeals by government and private nonprofit agencies which purport to do nothing but good, admonitions to viewers to engage in healthful behavior, and invocations of indisputable pieties. Any dramatic, sudden change in the nature and status of PSAs could cause serious stress and distress within the public service advertising nexus. Nonetheless, there are three signs of change: the presence of controversy surrounding some hitherto seemingly innocuous, consensual PSAs; the growing insistence on access to the airways; and the success of some wayward individuals and organizations in having their PSAs shown. We shall consider each phenomenon in turn.

RECENT CRITICISM OF PSAs

Despite the best efforts of the public service advertising nexus, PSAs are subject to increasing criticism. We discussed the problems of the antidrug campaign in Chapter 6. Additional objections could be leveled, if only by members of America's aging youth culture, to the way many antidrug PSAs lump marijuana together with dangerous narcotics. Another example is the campaign to stop teen-agers from dropping out of school—they are depicted in a PSA as contestants in a race encumbered by boots of lead. The premise has been criticized as "'based on a bad analysis of data and . . . largely misleading.'"[7] Indeed, the campaign is accused of giving dropouts a bad name and encouraging employers unnecessarily to require a high-school diploma. Of course, also explicit in the campaign, and worthy of scrutiny, is the assumption that schooling is desirable and schools useful institutions.

Even Smokey the Bear is not immune, for it is argued that the focus of PSAs featuring that animal is misconceived. There is apparently a body of professional opinion which regards some forest fires as necessary and desirable.

Furthermore, officials say that the fires usually are in remote areas where the trees would not be harvested for lumber, and that wildlife losses are generally greatly exaggerated."[8] Besides, forest fires are probably less threatening to the timber resources than some of the clear-cutting and indiscriminate logging engaged in by private companies. (Smokey the Bear, who had been retired because of age and grouchiness, recently died. As provided by Congressional resolution, his remains have been returned to Capitan, New Mexico, for proper disposition and the erection of a permanent memorial. The bear may be dead, but the symbol lives on in the shape of his erstwhile understudy, who has been given the same name and moved into Smokey's old quarters to receive the visits of schoolchildren. The power of PSAs in creating a national myth cannot be gainsaid.[9])

PSAs resulting from the traditional cooperation among the executive branch, the Advertising Council, and the networks are also coming under criticism. After President Ford's speech on inflation during which he announced his Whip Inflation Now (WIN) program, the New York *Times* reported that John S. Benton, president of the Benton and Bowles advertising agency, had written to the president offering the firm's services in building public support for the program. Benton and Bowles was planning to work with the Advertising Council, whose president, Robert P. Keim, had promised Ford that "'we [the Advertising Council] were ready to assist in any way possible.'"[10] Keim was also appointed by President Ford to the newly minted Citizens' Action Committee to Fight Inflation.

Subsequently, Congressman Benjamin S. Rosenthal (D., N.Y.), together with 27 other members of the House and Senate, sent letters to the Advertising Council and the presidents of the three networks protesting the Council's involvement in the WIN campaign. In the letter sent to the Council the legislators enumerated their reasons for disapproving of the Council's actions.

> (1) It [the WIN campaign] may persuade many citizens that the nation should, in fact, rally behind Mr. Ford's program, rather than seeking other more effective ways to combat inflation;
> (2) by placing primary responsibility for battling inflation on the consumer, rather than on special interests like those industries which raise prices in the face of declining demand, the "WIN" campaign may divert public attention away from many of the real causes of inflation;
> (3) it will distort the national debate on pressing economic matters by giving enormous publicity as well as support to the President's program while monopolizing "free public service" time and space;

(4) it will afford no exposure to the views of legislators like ourselves, even though the President's indecisive program has placed the primary responsibility for fighting inflation on the Congress;

(5) it makes the Ad Council a partisan propaganda arm of the executive branch, in plain violation of the Council's by-laws and at the expense of the basic First Amendment notion that America's press must be free from government influence so that it will expose the public fully and fairly to all sides of the important public issues.[11]

The congressmen also directed general criticism at the Council's other governmental campaigns: "We realize that the Ad Council has over the years served increasingly as the federal government's free advertising agency. Many Council campaigns . . . have a tendency to paper over ineffective governmental action in dealing with root social problems."[12]

SEEKING ACCESS

Many critics of PSAs demand an opportunity to make their views known to a larger audience, and the congressmen were no exception. Having expressed their indignation and concern, they sought access to the airwaves. The letter sent to the network presidents stated that the PSAs produced in conjunction with the WIN campaign should fall under the rubric of the fairness doctrine, since the president's proposals had generated vocal opposition from both ends of the political spectrum. The congressmen also complained that "it would be eminently unfair . . . to turn over the free airtime to the President's position because you regularly make free airtime available to the President whenever he deems it desirable to address the American people."[13] The congressmen concluded that if the networks were to air the Council's PSAs they would be obligated under the fairness doctrine to provide time to spokesmen for the opposing view, in particular for members of Congress and representatives of the Democratic party.

Congressman Rosenthal and his colleagues have continued their assault on the Advertising Council and the PSA nexus. Most recently, as we discussed in Chapter 1, they took on the Council-Commerce Department campaign to promote the free enterprise system. Indeed, the hearings held by Rosenthal's government operations subcommittee appear to have limited the government's financial investment and moderated the advocacy nature of that campaign.

Another attempt to use the fairness doctrine to force a station to allocate time for particular public service advertisements had been made by a group called the United People of Dayton, Ohio. In the fall of 1971, they filed a complaint with the FCC charging that Dayton station WLWD had "broadcast programs, public service announcement, and an editorial, all supporting the United Appeal . . . in Dayton, Ohio, and . . . afforded little opportunity for the presentation of contrasting views."[14] United People claimed that the broadcast campaign of the United Appeal constituted a controversial issue of public importance on the grounds that "the United Appeal does not allocate its funds in a proper relation to the most important needs of the community, that corporations do not give their fair share, and that the governing board of United Appeal is controlled by business leaders without representation of factory workers, poor people and youth."[15] The FCC agreed with the United People and so advised WLWD in order to assist the station in determining its fairness doctrine obligation in the forthcoming United Appeal campaign (the campaign which had caused the complaint was already over).

The ruling was narrow in application, concerning only the Dayton United Appeal. FCC Chairman, Dean Burch specifically delineated the limits of the ruling in his concurring opinion: "The Commission is not holding that henceforth announcements on behalf of the United Givers Appeal raise an issue of public importance throughout the nation. Nor is it holding that if there is [sic] within an area some people who disagree with announcements on behalf of such organizations as the Boy Scouts or the American Cancer Society, these announcements automatically fall within the strictures of the fairness doctrine."[16]

Rather than a shield behind which broadcasting executives can defend their restrictive practices, the fairness doctrine could be a sword used by critics of those policies to gain access to the television and radio stations for the expression of their point of view. The FCC's "United People of Dayton" decision offers a token of hope. More important are the actual requirements of the doctrine itself. The fairness doctrine is conventionally taken to require broadcasters to cover controversial public issues so as to provide fairly for the presentation of contrasting points of view. If an issue goes uncovered, many broadcast licensees apparently assume, fairness becomes irrelevant. If this were the extent of the fairness doctrine, broadcasting executives could continue to eschew controversy by eliminating controversial PSAs—even if forced to include United Fund appeals in this category. In fact, the fairness doctrine also imposes a duty on broadcasters to devote a reasonable amount of broadcast time to the treatment of public issues.[17] The doctrine could thus be used to spur such coverage, with PSAs as a possible mechanism. As might be expected, however, the provision has been treated by the FCC as an entreaty, and licensees are rarely rebuked, let alone punished, for failing to comply with it. Moreover, the latest FCC pronouncement on the fairness doctrine does not appear significantly to encourage the entrance of ideas and controversy in broadcasting, whether through paid advertising, PSAs, or any other means.[18]

INFILTRATION OF THE PSA NEXUS

The fairness doctrine remains of dubious worth for groups and individuals seeking to penetrate the PSA nexus, yet a modicum of infiltration has occurred recently. Individual and group entrepreneurs have produced PSAs outside the usual process and enjoyed some success in getting them shown. These achievers of access are of three kinds: individuals, activist groups, and newly created support structures.

Individual entrepreneurs can be represented by Robert M. Liebert, a child psychologist at the State University of New York at Stony Brook. He has produced spots with the conscious intention of influencing social behavior. They are designed "to demonstrate to children that there are non-violent, non-aggressive alternatives for solving problems."[19] One spot, distributed by the Broadcasting and Film Commission of the National Council of Churches and reportedly shown on all three networks, depicts two children (one boy, one girl) disagreeing over who should use the one swing in a playground. Finally, they decide to take turns. Cooperation and sharing breed contentment, is the message.

Stuart Hyde, chairman of the Department of Broadcast Communication Arts at San Francisco State University, is another successful individual entrepreneur. As part of a course he teaches at the prison, Hyde had inmates of San Quentin prepare, write, and present PSAs. Television executives are reportedly impressed with the results, which have been widely shown on local television stations. Hyde reports that "the self esteem of the men had increased significantly. Several former students are now out, and most have entered junior or senior colleges, some to study broadcasting."[20]

These two examples reveal that concerned, creative individuals can combine moxie, production expertise, and knowledge of the PSA funneling process to have their PSAs appear on local and network television. Without intending to denigrate either man, we must observe that their messages are perfectly consonant with the PSAs described throughout this book. The people appearing in Hyde's PSAs are uncommon; their messages are not. The prisoners primarily produced advertisements on drug abuse and employment for parolees. Antidrug messages are a staple of the PSA industry, and having ex-users deplore the habit is probably more effective than most such messages. No wonder the National Coordinating Council on Drug Education was interested in obtaining copies of the spots to use in its work.[21] Appeals for employment for parolees fit admirably into the consensus framework discussed in Chapter 9. The implications are that crime is the result of individual error, criminals are punished, following retribution comes forgiveness, and the economic system provides enough jobs for deserving able-bodied Americans.

Two of the inmate-produced PSAs were rejected by prison officials. In the first, a convict said: "If there's a pusher selling dope to my sister, the police better catch him before I do." Clearly such vigilantism cannot be countenanced.

A second PSA was rejected for obvious reasons: it began with an inmate berating society for the way men are treated in prison.

Activist groups have also sought access to the broadcast media with modest success. Indeed, although it may be all but impossible to persuade the networks to broadcast provocative, controversial PSAs, local stations are sometimes more receptive. Thus the Los Angeles NBC affiliate, KNBC, broadcast during 1974 approximately $1,690 worth of announcements for the Gay Community Services Center.[22] The station, after investigation, "determined that they [the Gay Community Services Center] do provide a service to a segment of the Southern California population and that they had a legitimate need to tell the audience of the service they provide."[23] There were few negative reactions from the community. This is not surprising, given the innocuous nature of the PSAs. They were 10- or 20-second announcements voiced over a color slide bearing the logo and telephone number of the organization. The announcements were purely informational, giving a brief list of the services available at the center or announcing an open house and ending with the statement that the center should be called for further information. No advocacy here, but a little status conferral for the gay liberation movement and a slight crack in the exclusion by the PSA nexus of any unconventional group from the airwaves.

The most important event in the PSA story is the recent arrival of organizations among whose specific purposes is to serve excluded groups by producing and distributing public service advertisements. They aim to provide a relatively stable, institutionalized challenge to the existing nexus and its dominance of the PSA funneling process. There appear to be several such organizations, including the Public Media Center in San Francisco and Washington, D.C. (formerly Public Interest Communications), the Media Access Project, Inc., in Washington, D.C., and, in Los Angeles, Public Communications Inc. and its apparent successor in producing ads, the Public Advertising Council. Aiming directly at the interests of low- and middle-income consumers, Public Communications, Inc., during its heyday devised radio commercials telling "people not to put up with telephone harassment over debts, how to collect on overbooked airline flights, about the food stamp program and about buying drugs by generic name to save money."[24] These PSAs are liable to disrupt consensus, provoke controversy, and stimulate political participation, for they suggest that the typical American is uninformed, deceived, harassed, and exploited; that the perpetrators of such iniquities are established institutions and authorities; and that information previously denied, action people may never have considered or believed conceivable, can improve the situation. Similarly, Public Communications, Inc., "produced messages for television on auto safety, deceptive advertising for pain remedies, water pollution, drug abuse and voter registration . . . the Public Advertising Council . . . has produced radio spots for the Discharge Upgrading Project criticizing punitive discharges of Vietnam veterans; radio spots for the Citizens Action Project on discriminatory credit and loan practices; radio and TV ads for the National

Sharecropper Fund on the problems of rural farming; and a TV ad for the People's Bicentennial Commission on the atrophy of the Bill of Rights."[25]

On an annual budget of less than $100,000, the Public Media Center has prepared television and radio messages for the United Farm Workers, Network Against Psychiatric Assault, the NAACP Legal Defense Fund, Public Advocates, Movement for Social Justice, the Women's Coalition for Health Rights, and similar groups. For Friends of the Earth, Environmental Action, and other groups, it has been extensively involved in energy issues–questioning the safety and efficiency of nuclear reactors (based on the theme "Nuclear Power Is a Terrible Way to Go," usually written on a tombstone). It is also trying to show how the energy crisis was caused by long-term mismanagement on the part of the energy industry and government.

On behalf of the Center for Growth Alternatives, a prestigious outfit which includes on its board former Oregon governor Tom L. McCall, the Public Media Center has undertaken a campaign on growth and resource consumption with the theme "We Can't Grow on Like This."[26] It is seeking funds "for similar campaigns on population growth (for Zero Population Growth), returnable containers (for Environmental Action), and nutrition (for Center for Science in the Public Interest)."[27] These are all groups whose contentions, even contentious messages, are almost completely barred from the broadcast media.

The Public Advertising Council in cooperation with the Public Media Center, is devising a program on economic alternatives to balance or counter the Ad Council's federally supported campaign on the American economy we discussed previously. The PAC has received seed money and is trying to assemble a coalition of interested public organizations. The PSAs would discuss the broader range of alternatives of the American economy. As this campaign reaches fruition, the resultant PSAs may not enjoy wide circulation on television, but they will make it more difficult for the networks and stations to accept the Ad Council-government commercials.

Two organizations, working with the Public Advertising Council, have achieved conspicuous success in placing their PSAs on television. Their examples are instructive.

Action for Children's Television devised three PSAs. Two featured Mary Tyler Moore explicitly urging better programs and fewer commercials on children's television. In the second she is quite vehement: "It disturbs me that much of children's television is a way to sell kids things they don't need." The third PSA, entitled "Undivided Attention," shows a child sitting, apparently watching television. Viewers hear the following:

> If you had your children's undivided attention twenty-two hours a week, what would you teach them?
>
> How to read and write?
>
> That animals are friends?

> How to get along with other children?
> That too much sugar can be bad for your teeth?
> That it's wrong to kill another person?
>
> We are Action for Children's Television and we're working to improve what children see on tv. But we can't do it alone. For more information on how you can help, write. . . .It's time you got into the act!

Peggy Charron of ACT wrote to the heads of the broadcast standards divisions of the three networks and then showed them the spots. CBS rejected all three PSAs. ABC and NBC both accepted "Undivided Attention" and gave it prominent play, including prime time. Had the time been purchased, the estimated cost would have been $95,000 on each network. ABC notified ACT of its decision and indicated when the PSA would be shown. ACT had to contact NBC to learn of that network's actions.

The reasons two of the three networks accorded favorable treatment to the ACT commercial are not difficult to unravel. From their point of view they accepted the least provocative of the three PSAs. Even then, a somewhat controversial line was changed from "Sugar is bad for your health," to "Too much sugar can be bad for your teeth." Moreover, it is probably in the networks' legitimate, not to mention political, interest to cooperate as much as possible with ACT. Nor should we overlook the initiative of ACT's Peggy Charron, whose previous dealings with the networks revealed her to be a formidable antagonist. Because of her past experiences, she knew which strategically located network executives to contact. And clearly the decision to show or not to show the ACT PSAs was made at the executive level.

From ACT's point of view, the PSA was an effective publicity and recruiting device: it elicited at least 3,000 cards and letters to the box number provided. What it did not do was adequately communicate ACT's message to viewers: ACT's indictment of children's television and its bill of particulars against excessive commercialism were still denied access to viewers by the networks.

Perhaps the most success at persuading local radio and television stations to air its messages has been achieved by the Safe Return Amnesty Committee, an organization working to obtain universal, unconditional amnesty for all categories of war resisters, including army deserters and draft evaders. In conjunction with the Public Advertising Council an appropriate PSA was devised. It featured film star Burt Lancaster sitting behind his desk, apparently at home. As the camera fades up on him he removes his glasses and speaks.

> Thousands of young Americans had to leave homes and families rather than participate in the Vietnam War. They want to come home, but President Ford's "Clemency Program" would brand them as second-class citizens. War resisters need amnesty, not clemency.

> Let's really put the war behind us and bring all the boys home, now! You can help. Contact SAFE RETURN, Madison Square Station, New York, N.Y., 10010

The 30-second spot, which cost Safe Return $5,000 (including copies), reportedly "has been aired by nearly one hundred and fifty TV stations from coast to coast. At the same time, PSAs for radio have been distributed to the 3,900 AM-FM radio stations in the U.S. A sizeable percentage of these stations are also airing the message."[28] Somewhat to the surprise of the organizers of Safe Return, their greatest success has been with smaller television stations, particularly those in the south and southwest. The strongest resistance occurred in New York City.

How do we explain this success, especially with television stations one might expect to be both politically conservative and reluctant to air controversy? The PSA format is low-key, with the speaker sitting calmly behind his desk. Lancaster is dignified and has high prestige (his most recent television role was that of Moses). The message urges no explicit action from viewers other than contacting Safe Return. President Ford's Clemency Board had apparently launched a media effort with PSAs featuring board members Father Theodore Hesburgh, president of Notre Dame University, and General Lewis Walt. Their messages urged resisters to accept the president's program.[29] Thus stations might feel a responsibility to show Safe Return's PSA on grounds of fairness and balance. Besides, the clemency program was soon to expire, so equal time for differing opinions would not likely be a continuing issue. Finally, Lancaster appears previously to have been featured in a PSA prepared by the American Civil Liberties Union and the National Council of Churches dealing with clemency but not advocating unconditional amnesty, so there may have been some confusion in the minds of busy station personnel about organizations and PSAs.

On the other hand, the Safe Return PSA was controversial, advocated an unpopular viewpoint, and opposed the Ford administration's policy. Since the president's program was shortly to expire, local stations could have avoided having to show Safe Return's message by obfuscation and delay. Yet, in comparison to other controversial PSAs, it was widely shown. This success was no accident, but the result of a conscious campaign. Letters from Burt Lancaster, members of Congress, and the Public Advertising Council were sent with a copy of the PSA's script to all television stations in the United States. A stamped postcard was enclosed containing the station's name and call letters and asking how many times the PSA would be run. This approach was combined with a mailing to members and supporters of Families of Resisters for Amnesty (FORA). Recipients of the letter were told that the purpose of the PSA was "to focus public pressure on the new 94th Congress to recognize and correct the glaring inadequacies and the injustice of Ford's Clemency and Re-Entry Programs."[30] A telephone network was organized with members calling their local stations asking station managers whether they knew about the PSA and would be willing to show it, thus capitalizing on the desire of stations to show locally relevant PSAs. If interest was expressed, a kit of materials including a copy of the PSA was sent from Safe Return headquarters in New York City. Members and supporters of the organization and of FORA were then asked to monitor their local stations to ensure that the PSA was aired. Subsequently, recipients of the organization's newsletter were urged to call their local television and radio stations to ask them if they had aired the PSA.[31]

The obvious assumptions behind these tactics are that excluded groups need to ally with other groups and individuals around the country and have them try to place the spots in conjunction with the national headquarters. This tactic may be especially effective in the light of the questions on the Federal Communications Commission's revised license renewal form concerning local versus national spots.

Supplementing the tactics of mass mailing and organizing volunteers to contact their local stations were the written materials sent to the local stations. They appealed for showing the PSA on the grounds of reason, fairness, decency, and prestige. The carefully restrained, unthreatening letter sent out under Burt Lancaster's name reads as follows:

> The enclosed public service announcement concerns an issue which I believe to be of major importance to our country; whether amnesty should be given to those who refused to serve in Vietnam.
>
> The fact that I'm featured in the announcement is one indication of how intensely I personally feel about this issue. While I realize that many Americans honestly believe that amnesty would be wrong for our country, I think that the public is served by the expression of all points of view.
>
> I know that the Public Advertising Council and the Safe Return Amnesty Committee are reputable, non-profit, organizations. They are, in my opinion, providing a real service to our nation.
>
> It seems to me that, to date, the functioning of President Ford's "earned re-entry" program has received quite a bit more attention than have the views of those who favor amnesty.
>
> I respectfully urge you to find time in your station's schedule of public-service time, to air the enclosed announcement. Both those who already support amnesty and those who want further information are entitled to a presentation of a pro-amnesty point of view.

Despite its success with local stations, the Safe Return Amnesty Committee accomplished little with the television networks, all of which had reportedly shown Clemency Board announcements. Safe Return's organizers considered filing a formal complaint with the Federal Communications Commission protesting the refusal of the networks to air its amnesty PSA, but decided it would not be a profitable use of resources.

As exemplified by the Safe Return Amnesty Committee case, organizations such as the Public Media Center, the Public Advertising Council, and Public Communications, Inc, pose the most significant challenge to the domination of the airwaves for public service advertising by the nexus consisting of the Advertising Council, the presidential administration, advertising agencies, and allied (or dependent) "charitable" beneficiaries. Because they have a modicum of organizational stability, the Public Media Center, Public Communications, Inc., and the Public Advertising Council are able to channel the needs of organizations and individuals who take issue with the prevailing orthodoxies and myths perpetrated by the PSA nexus. They possess the talent and technical skills to produce PSAs, and they have devised tactics to facilitate access for some of the PSAs they develop. They are growing yet they lack sustained and sustaining funding, and they cannot compel television and radio stations to accept their messages. In truth, their existence seems precarious, their threat still not significant.[32]

NOTES

1. James N. Rosenau, *Citizenship Between Elections* (New York: The Free Press, 1974), p. 437.
2. Murray Edelman, "Language, Myths and Rhetoric," *Society* 12 (July-August 1975): 18.
3. We have culled several of the ideas that follow from Joan Huber and William H. Form, *Income and Ideology* (New York: The Free Press, 1973), pp. 154-63. The book makes no reference to PSAs.
4. Ibid., p. 157.
5. Sidney Verba and Norman H. Nie, *Participation in America: Political Democracy and Social Equality* (New York: Harper and Row, 1972), pp. 252-59.
6. Letter from Jay E. Gerber, assistant general attorney, NBC, to Thomas D. Ensign, Safe Return Amnesty Committee, January 31, 1975.
7. " Are They Really Better off in School?" New York *Times*, May 7, 1972.
8. For such thoughts see Thomas Asher, "Smokey the Bear and the Ad Council," *More* March 1972, p. 1.
9. Letter to the authors from Congressman Harold Runnels (D., N.M.) January 21, 1975; see also "New Mexico Plans a Park to Honor Smokey the Bear," New York *Times*, May 4, 1975, and "Retirement Next for Smokey Bear," Durham *Morning Herald*, May 1 and "Retirement at Home Out for Smokey," August 10, 1975.
10. "Advertising Council to Aid Ford's Drive," New York *Times*, October 9, 1974.
11. *Congressional Record*, December 4, 1974, E6955.
12. Ibid.
13. Ibid.
14. 32 FCC 2d (1973), p. 124.
15. Ibid. See also "Nothing Safe from Fairness," *Broadcasting* 81 (October 25, 1971): 50-51.
16. 32 FCC 2d, p. 127.
17. See 13 FCC, *Report* "On Editorializing," p. 1249.
18. 48 FCC 2d. p. 1 *Fairness Report*, (1974).
19. "What Sort of Behavior Control Should TV Impose on Children: Violence or Harmony?" New York *Times*, August 18, 1974. For a more detailed account, see the unpublished paper by Robert M. Liebert, Joyce N. Sprafkin, and Rita Wicks Poulos, "Selling Cooperation to Children," presented before the Advertising Research Foundation, November 1974.

20. Personal communication to the authors from Stuart Hyde, January 28, 1975.

21. According to Hyde, the Council did nothing with the spots.

22. Letter to the authors from Howard D. Strum, manager, Public Affairs, KNBC-TV, Los Angeles, California (February 10, 1975).

23. Ibid.

24. "Inside Stuff-Radio-TV," *Variety,* July 18, 1973.

25. Henry Weinstein,"... And Selling Truth," *Ramparts* 13 (December 1974/January 1975): 27.

26. "De-Growth Outfit Eyeing Free Media Ads vs. 'Buy' Yen," *Variety,* July 2, 1975.

27. Letter to the authors from Alan Lewis, Public Media Center, April 3, 1975.

28. *Amnesty Report* 6 (Spring 1975): 1.

29. Ibid.

30. Letter from Ed Sowders of Families of Resisters for Amnesty (FORA) to members and supporters of the organization, December 9, 1974.

31. *Amnesty Report* 6 (Spring 1975): 3.

32. But perhaps we are too pessimistic. In June 1976, the Media Access Project, representing 66 organizations throughout the United States, and five members of Congress, including Benjamin Rosenthal, filed a petition with the Federal Communications Commission seeking drastic changes in the public service advertising process. Among the most significant changes requested are the following:

> The broadcaster shall air at least three public service announcements during each two consecutive hours of broadcast service, including prime time. . . . At least 25 percent of all PSA's shall be local in origin. . . . The licensee shall make available to local organizations the use of its facilities . . . for the production of PSA's. . . .No more than 20 percent of the PSA's aired by a broadcast licensee, including a network . . . may be produced by or in cooperation with a single entity or organization, including the Advertising Council. . . . A licensee's policy of refusing to accept any PSA's which might be considered controversial, or which might conceivable [*sic*] give rise to fairness doctrine obligations, will not be considered to be operating in the public interest.

See Media Access Project, Washington, D.C., *Fact Sheet and Summary of Petition to Institute a Notice of Inquiry and Proposed Rulemaking on the Airing of Public Service Announcements by Broadcast Licensees.*

CHAPTER

13

CONCLUSIONS

Proponents and purveyors of public service advertisements may contend that their modest purpose is to encourage activities which benefit the public; to increase donations to charity; to provide information about governmental services; and to help people protect themselves against common hazards to life and limb (assuming government is not such a hazard). Political behavior and participation are not their affair.

Such an argument is superficially persuasive. Certainly, since PSAs are apparently deliberately nonpartisan and noncontroversial and are not sponsored by political parties, it is no surprise that they never urge viewers to participate in any overtly political activity except voting.

We respond first that politics and participation should not be so casually disregarded and cannot be so narrowly defined, and second, that although PSAs may not be political in intent, many of them are political in effect. PSAs reach a massive audience and create awareness, channel predispositions, and reinforce behavior. It is therefore reasonable to assume that the values they convey will subliminally affect viewers and enter their subconscious.

Our perspective is best expressed by George Gerbner's observation "that communication is the environment of social behavior rather than just specific acts, utterances and campaigns. The most profound effects of communication can be found not in making sales, getting votes, influencing opinions and changing attitudes, but in the selective maintenance of relatively stable structures of images and associations that stem from institutional structures and policies and that define the common perspectives of a society."[1] Specifically, for their viewers, many PSAs promote a deceptive societal consensus; encourage the questionable feeling that governmental and established private nonprofit agencies are instrumentally capable, deserving of affect and support; and, instead of political activity, promote pseudo-participation.

We do not, of course, suggest that PSAs have the capacity single-handedly to determine successfully the direction, intensity, duration, and extent of the American people's political perceptions and participation. Many variables, of which media content is only one, affect behavior. And PSAs, although important, are only one part of media content. No matter how benevolent government appears in PSAs, public confidence in America's rulers and institutions is likely to be more immediately influenced by economic dislocation, and by incompetence, venality, and malevolence in high office. Moreover, whatever immediate impact each individual PSA could have may be vitiated through the inadequate pretesting, inept deployment, and lack of follow-up we have chronicled. Even if these inefficiencies are overcome—the manifest intent of most of what there is of academic writing on PSAs—we would not argue that PSAs are or will be overwhelmingly important in determining the future of political activity in the United States.

And yet, events come and go; PSAs persist. At a rate of some 47 billion television impressions annually, they are, we believe, a significant part of media content and more influential than most of it. They are influential because they appear as a constant barrage of messages different in subject but similar in political effects; they use the panoply of tried (albeit not necessarily true) persuasive techniques developed in commercial advertising; and they do not appear overtly to sell viewers products. Indeed, because they often seem to be directed at the viewers' best interests, they are less liable to evoke the conventional defenses with which we customarily protect ourselves against commercial advertising. PSAs depict societal and individual problems as unrelated to politics and propose nonpolitical solutions. The funneling system is organized to deny air time to groups or organizations which could present different perspectives, which might introduce political considerations, urge political action, and define political activity so as to legitimate it in schools and workplaces. If "for most citizens the world of politics is remote, bewildering, and meaningless, having no direct relation to daily concerns about jobs or family life,"[2] public service advertisements, and the people responsible for them, bear some of the responsibility for making it so.

NOTES

1. George Gerbner, "Communication and Social Environment," *Scientific American* 227 (September 1972): 158.

2. We attribute this statement to Walter Dean Burnham, who responds, "Si non è vero, è ben trovato."

INDEX

ABOUT THE AUTHORS

DAVID L. PALETZ teaches Political Science at Duke University. He received his Ph.D. at UCLA and has been a Guest Scholar at the Brookings Institution and an American Political Science Association Congressional Fellow.

Professor Paletz is the author of numerous monographs and articles on such topics as four-letter threats to authority, television coverage of presidential nominating conventions, the Senate Watergate hearings as television drama, how the media support local governmental authority, the presidency, congressional campaigns, and the striving after success in academe. His work has appeared in such publications as the *Journal of Politics, Political Science Quarterly, Public Opinion Quarterly, Polity,* and *Film Quarterly*.

The recipient of a Rockefeller Humanities Fellowship, Dr. Paletz is presently writing a book advocating press freedom from responsibility.

ROBERTA E. PEARSON graduated from Duke University magna cum laude in 1974. She is presently a graduate student in political science at Yale University.

DONALD L. WILLIS attended Duke University and graduated cum laude in 1973 with a B.A. in Political Science. He was project director for the Youth-grant from the National Endowment for the Arts and Humanities, which advanced the completion of this book. Mr. Willis presently resides in San Francisco where he is involved in pharmaceutical work.

RELATED TITLES
Published by
Praeger Special Studies

CHILDREN'S TELEVISION: An Analysis of Programming and Advertising
F. Earle Barcus
with Rachel Wolkin

CITIZENS' GROUPS AND BROADCASTING
Donald L. Guimary

GETTING TO SESAME STREET: Origins of the Children's Television Workshop
Richard M. Polsky

TELEVISION AS A CULTURAL FORCE
edited by Richard Adler
and Douglass Cater

TELEVISION AS A SOCIAL FORCE: New Approaches to TV Criticism
edited by Douglass Cater
and Richard Adler

TELEVISION IN THE CORPORATE INTEREST
Richard Brunce